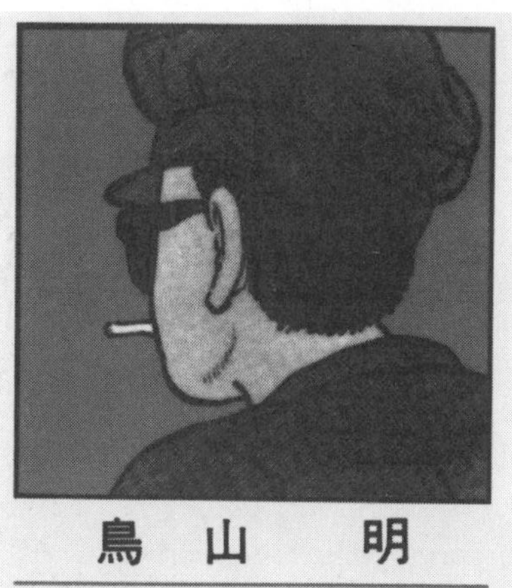

鳥山 明

The setting for **Dragon Ball** has a sort of Chinese feel to it but it's not necessarily the real China. Exactly where it takes place is uncertain. The overall story is very simple, but I'd like to keep making up more details and illustrations as I go along. This way, I can draw anything I want to and enjoy the tension and excitement of figuring out what I'll draw next.

–Akira Toriyama, 1985

Widely known all over the world for his playful, innovative storytelling and humorous, distinctive art style, **Dragon Ball** creator Akira Toriyama is also known in his native Japan as the creator of the wildly popular **Dr. Slump**, his previous manga series about the adventures of a mad scientist and his android "daughter." His hit series **Dragon Ball** ran from 1984 to 1995 in Shueisha's weekly **Shônen Jump** magazine. He is also known for his design work on video games such as **Dragon Warrior**, **Chrono Trigger** and **Tobal No. 1**. His recent manga works include **Cowa**, **Kajika**, **Sand Land**, and the short self-parody **Neko Majin Z**. He lives with his family in Tokyo, Japan.

DRAGON BALL VOL. 1

This graphic novel, number 1 in a series of 42, contains the monthly comic series DRAGON BALL #1 through #6 in their entirety.

STORY AND ART BY
AKIRA TORIYAMA

ENGLISH ADAPTATION BY
GERARD JONES

Translation/Mari Morimoto
Touch-Up Art & Lettering/Wayne Truman
Cover Design/Hidemi Sahara
Graphics & Layout/Sean Lee
Edited by/Trish Ledoux
Collected Edition Edited by/Jason Thompson
V.P. of Sales & Marketing/Rick Bauer

Managing Editor/Annette Roman
Editor-in-Chief/Hyoe Narita
Publisher/Seiji Horibuchi

PARENTAL ADVISORY
Dragon Ball contains images and themes that may be unsuitable for young children. It is recommended for ages 13 and up.

Printed in Canada

Published by Viz Communications, Inc.
P.O. Box 77010 • San Francisco, CA 94107

10 9 8 7
First printing, August 2000
Fifth printing, August 2001
Sixth printing, May 2002
Seventh printing, August 2002
Vizit us at our World Wide Web site at www.vizkids.com!

VIZ GRAPHIC NOVEL

DRAGON BALL

Vol. 1

DB: 1 of 42

STORY AND ART BY
AKIRA TORIYAMA

DRAGON BALL 1

LONG, LONG AGO, IN A DEEP, DARK FOREST FAR FROM CIVILIZATION, BEYOND A TOWERING RANGE OF...WELL, YOU GET THE IDEA. IT'S THE KIND OF PLACE A STORY LIKE THIS HAS TO BEGIN...
CHEE-CHEE!
HEY, BRO! WUZZUP ?!
GRRON GRRON

Tale 1

Bloomers and the Monkey king

HNNN-
NNNN...

PREPARE
TO
DIE!!!

poing

NYAH
!!!

NO
ESCAPE
!!!

BWONG

GLOMP

HI-
YAA
!!!

HWNN

BAKOKOKOKOKO...!!

LA-DE-DE-DE-DUM...

PF 8801

twee twee twee...

GOT TO BE RIGHT... AROUND... *HERE*...

peep peep

OR MAYBE A LITTLE MORE TO THE WEST... ?

ANYWAY, I'M CLOSE... I'M CLOSE !

BULMA

TURBO

PF 8801

BWOOOM

OH, YEAH! FISH! I FORGOT ABOUT *FISH*!

ROOOOARRR...

PUSH

plip
plip

HUH ?!

WA HA HA!! GOT YA, YA DUMB-BUTT LITTLE MONKEY!!

HEY-
YAA
!!!

BLASH
SHP

HEH
HEH!
BURBLE
BURBLE...

DONK!!

WOTTA
CATCH!!
WOTTA
CATCH!!
ZHH ZHH ZHH...

VRRROOOM...

HUH? WAZZAT... ?

ZHZHZH...

WAA !!!

BAOO..M!!

TURBO

PF8801

WAA !!!!

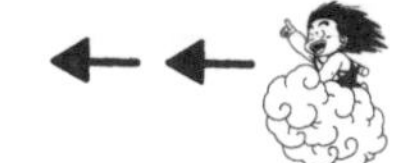

OHHH... OH... WHOA...
WATCH WHERE YOU'RE *GOING*, YOU ROAD-BLOCK!!

SO...A *MONSTER*, EH?!!
TRYIN' TO SNATCH MY *PREY* FROM ME, EH?!!

WELL... YOU'RE NOT... GETTIN' AWAY... WITH MY FISH...!!
GNNNG!!
WHAT--?!
WHAT--?!
HYOH!!!!
DGOG

NOW, C'MON AND *FIGHT* !!!
C'MON!! FIGHT!! *C'MON* !!!

PAM PAM
SQUELCH IT, PEE-WEE!!

YEESH... NOW A HIDEOUS DEMON EMERGES FROM THE MONSTER!

NGH... HUF... UHH... OOF...
TURBO

WHUH WAS THAT?!! WHAT'RE YOU, A WITCH?!
OWW-EEE!! OW!! OW!!

!!

NOW, DEMON... PREPARE TO DIE!!!

I'M NOT A DEMON!! I'M A HUMAN!!!
WAIT! WHOA! TIME OUT!!
BULMA

WH-WHAT ARE YOU...?! WHY AREN'T YOU DEAD?!
YEE... GODS...!!
HA! DUMMY! STUPID! Y'THINK YOU CAN HURT ME?! WITH LITTLE OWCHIES LIKE THAT!? HAH!

HUH?! A HUMAN ?!
REALLY ?!
YES, SILLY!! I'M JUST LIKE YOU!!
TAKE A GANDER !
...
BULMA

DON'T MAKE A MOVE!
NOT VERY TRUSTING, ARE YOU.

VIP VIP VIP
BULMA

YOU'RE KINDA LIKE ME... BUT THERE'S SOMETHING... DIFFERENT...
YOU SEEM KINDA... SOFTER... AND BUMPIER!

WULL DUH, BRAINIAC !
YOU'RE A BIG HE-MAN AN' I'M A CUTE LI'L GIRL!

G-GIRL ?!
YOU MEAN... FEMALE ?!

MY DEAD GRAMPA ALWAYS TOLD ME...
"IF YOU EVER MEET A GIRL, TREAT HER NICE."

WELL, THEN... DON'T YOU THINK YOU SHOULD GET STARTED ?

HEH-LOH !!
SURELY YOU'VE SEEN A GIRL BEFORE!
I NEVER SAW ANOTHER HUMAN BEFORE!

MAN... THAT IS WEIRD...
pwik pwik

HUH ?
SO FEMALES DON'T HAVE TAILS, EH...?

SO WHAT IS THAT MONSTER ANYWAY? HOW'D YOU CATCH IT?
THAT "MONSTER" HAPPENS TO BE MY CAR. PEOPLE MAKE THEM.

PROB'LY THINKS WEARING THAT PHONY TAIL MAKES HIM LOOK LIKE ONE HAPPENIN' DUDE!
SNORT
WHAT A GOON !

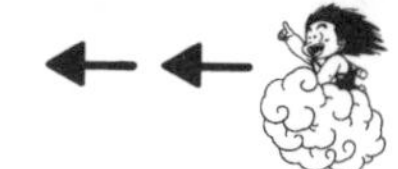

SO THIS IS A CAR! I'VE HEARD OF 'EM IN STORIES...
HUH. IT LOOKS TOUGH... BUT IT AIN'T MUCH!

WHOA, WHOA, WAIT...ARE YOU FROM "CIVILIZATION" ?!
WELL... LET'S JUST SAY I'M FROM WAY FAR WEST.

YOU'RE PRETTY STRONG FOR A RUNT.
HAW HAW !
GRAMPA TRAINED ME GOOD!

HE MAY BE A FREAK...
...BUT I CAN USE THAT STRENGTH OF HIS!

COME OVER TO MY PLACE! YOU'RE A GIRL, SO I'LL FEED YOU!
AS LONG AS THAT'S ALL YOU DO...

WAIT HERE A SEC...
KREEE...
NOT MUCH FOR HOME REPAIR, ARE YOU?

GRAMPA, LOOK! IT'S A FEMALE! A HUMAN FEMALE IN OUR HOUSE!
HUH ?

THAT'S IT!!!!
THE DRAGON BALL!!!!

Wa-HOOOO!!!
I *KNEW* IT!! MY DETECTOR WAS RIGHT *ON*!!
BOMP

HEY!! LEGGO O' *GRAMPA*!!!
THAT WAS HIS LAST POSSESSION!! EVEN *GIRLS* AREN'T ALLOWED TO TOUCH IT!!

WELL... I GUESS I HAFTA LET YOU IN ON MY LI'L SECRET...
SHFF
SHFF
?

VOILÀ!!

AAA!!!
MORE GRAMPA!! *TWO* MORE GRAMPAS!!

I FOUND ONE IN MY CELLAR. I HAD NO IDEA WHAT IT WAS...
...AND NEITHER DID ANYONE ELSE I ASKED.
THEY'RE CALLED "DRAGON BALLS."
Y'MEAN... SOME POOR DRAGON...?
NO, NO... TEE HEE...
SO I DID SOME RESEARCH...AND I FOUND THIS OLD, OLD, OLD STORY THAT DESCRIBED THEM.
THERE WERE ORIGINALLY SEVEN DRAGON BALLS, AND EACH OF THEM GLOWS WITH THE LIGHT OF THE TINY STARS INSIDE...FROM ONE STAR TO SEVEN...
GRAMPA HAS FOUR STARS IN 'IM!
THEN THAT'S "SŪSHINCHŪ"... THE FIRST ONE I FOUND WAS "ARUSHINCHŪ"... "TWO-STAR-BALL"...
AND AFTER WEEKS SEARCHING THE NORTH VALLEY...
I FINALLY FOUND "ŌSHINCHŪ"... "FIVE-STAR-BALL"!
YOU'RE COLLECTIN' THEM?
ALMOST HALF WAY THERE! BUT IT WON'T BE NO CAKE-WALK FROM HERE ON...
BULMA
97

...AND YOU CHANT JUST THE RIGHT CHANT...TO SUMMON...

...SHENLONG... THE DRAGON GOD!! HE'LL GRANT YOU ANY WISH! BUT ONLY ONE!!

TEE HEE HEE...AND I'VE ALREADY SETTLED ON A WISH!
AT FIRST I WANTED A LIFETIME SUPPLY OF STRAWBERRIES... BUT NOW I THINK I'M GONNA GO FOR A SUPER-CUTE BOYFRIEND!!
...

SO THAT'S THE DEAL!
NOW GIMME THE *SŪSHINCHŪ*, PLEASE!!

NO!! NO *WAY*!!
THIS IS TH' ONLY GRAMPA I GOT LEFT!!

COME *ON*, YOU CHEAP-SKATE!!
WHAT ARE *YOU* GONNA DO WITH IT, HUH?!!
NYAAH!!

OH, *I* GET IT!! YOU NAUGHTY BOY!
YOU WANT SOMETHIN' IN EXCHANGE!
?

OKAY!
BUT JUST ONE QUICK LI'L FEEL ♡

WHY WOULD I WANNA FEEL YOUR DIRTY BUTT?!
MY BUTT IS *NOT* DIRTY!!!

OKAY, OKAY!! YOU CAN *HELP* ME WITH MY QUEST!!
GRAMPA TOLD YOU TO BE NICE TO GIRLS, RIGHT?!

O-KAAAY... BUT I'M *NOT* GIVIN' YOU GRAMPA!
FINE! FINE! I'LL JUST BORRY IT AT THE VERY END, 'KAY?

YOU DON'T HAVE ANYTHING *BETTER* TO DO, DO YA?!
YOU'RE A *HE*-MAN! YOU'RE S'POSED TO *LOVE* QUESTS!
YOUR... QUEST... ?

HEE HEE HEEEE... PERFECT! IDIOT-LAD'LL BE THE IDEAL BODYGUARD... AND HE DOESN'T NEED TO KNOW THAT ONCE THE WISH IS GRANTED...
...THE DRAGON BALLS FLY OFF TO THE ENDS OF THE EARTH!!

HO HO HO!
I'M NOT JUST A PRETTY FACE, Y'KNOW!
ALTHOUGH I CERTAINLY AM THAT!

ALL-RIGH*TEE*!!
LET THE ADVENTURE *BEGIN*!! YIPPEE!!
BUT HOW'RE WE GONNA FIND THE OTHER BALLS IF YOU DON'T EVEN KNOW WHERE THEY ARE?

FEAST YOUR PEEPERS ON *THIS*!
peep peep
?

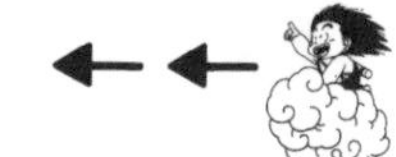

peep peep
IT'S MY BALL DETECTOR !!
I NOTICED THAT THE BALLS GIVE OFF A FAINT ELECTROMAGNETIC PULSE, SO I CONSTRUCTED IT! SEE, THESE THREE IN THE MIDDLE ARE THE ONES WE HAVE RIGHT NOW, AND...

THE NEXT CLOSEST IS...
...TO THE WEST! ABOUT 1,200 KILOMETERS !!
?
?
I DON'T GET IT.

YOU WRECKED MY CAR, SO I'LL JUST HAVE TO TAKE OUT A NEW ONE.
BY THE WAY, WHAT'S YOUR NAME?
BULMA
ME ?

I'M GOKU.
SON GOKU !

HOW 'BOUT YOU ?
I'M... BULMA...

DOESN'T THAT MEAN "BLOOMERS" ?! HAW!!
SHUT UP !! I DIDN'T PICK IT!!!

HA HA HA! "BLOOMERS" !!
SHNAK
LITTLE TWERP... !
I HATE LITTLE TWERPS !

HE MADE ME FORGET WHICH...
OH YEAH... NUMBER 9!!

TA-DAH!

AW-*RIIGHT* !!

LET'S *RIDE* !!

EEEE-YAGGA !!!

I ***KNEW*** IT!!! YOU ***ARE*** A WITCH!!!

BULMA

AF4029

PSULE

GET OVER IT, APE-BOY!
NOW SWING YOUR TAIL UP HERE!
EVERYBODY IN THE CITY'S GOT HOI-POI CAPSULES!
...??
tng tng
SPUT-PUT-PUTTT...
VROOM

EEE-YOW-WOW!!!
VWOOM

TH-THIS THING G-GOES EVEN FASTER THAN I CAN RUN!! I DIDN'T THINK THAT WAS POSSIBLE!!!
HEY!! WATCH WHAT YOU'RE GRABBIN' ONTO!!
pwop
...

20 MINUTES LATER...

ZWEEEEEEEE...

BWEEEN

SKREEEE...

PHEW!

MAN, THAT WAS INCREDIBLE!! YOU ACTUALLY MADE US FLY!!
Y-YEAH... PR-PRETTY GOOD, HUH...?
I DIDN'T THINK THE HILL'D BE THAT STEEP...!!
B-BUMP
B-BUMP

'SCUSE ME FOR A SEC!
BE RIGHT BACK!
HUH?! WHY?! WHERE YOU GOIN'?!

YOU MEAN YOU GOTTA PEE?
DON'T YOU HAVE ANY IDEA WHAT A LADY MEANS WHEN SHE SAYS "'SCUSE ME," YOU OAF?!

WELL?!
WHY'S SHE GOTTA PEE WAY OVER THERE? WHY CAN'T SHE DO IT RIGHT HERE, LIKE A NORMAL PERSON?

WHA-- ?!
AAIIEEEE
HOO !!
NOW WHAT'S WRONG ?
I HOPE HER WEENIE DIDN'T GET BIT BY A SNAKE!
JNG JNG JNG
WHO ARE YOU?!! PART OF HER PACK?!!
NAH, I JUST MET HER. YOU A FRIEND O' HERS?
UH... UH... UH...!!

WHY WOULD HE TIE ME UP ?
FUNNY...
YEAH...FRIEND... THAT'S IT! BWA-HA-HA! LOOK, THERE'S SOMETHING I HAVE TO DISCUSS WITH HER IN PRIVATE, OKAY? YOU JUST WAIT RIGHT HERE!
WAAA... EEEEK !!
?

FLAP FLAP
IT'S BEEN FAR TOO LONG SINCE I'VE TASTED FEMALE HUMAN FLESH! BWA-HA-HA!!
DON'T TAKE TOO LONG, OKAY?
WHA... WHA...

BWA-HA-HA--
IMBECILE!
DOLT!
OH, SO NOW SHE WANTS ME TO RESCUE HER!

RESCUE ME, IDIOT !!!!
WHAT ARE YOU WAITING FOR?!!

I WISH SHE'D MAKE UP HER MIND!
TUG TUG

SOME FRIEND *HE* IS!
HOW'M I GONNA DO THIS...? I CAN'T FL...
HEY !!

THAT'S IT!!!
VSSSH

HWA

IF I CAN JUST REMEMBER...

LESSEE...I THINK SHE TWISTED *THIS*...

PUT PUT PUT PUTT
YOW-WAH !!
WOBBLE WOBBLE

HOT *DOG*!! IT'S MOVIN' !!!
ALL RIGHT!! ALL RIGHT!!
AF4029
CAPS 9

VROOM!!
AIII~
CAPSULE
9
BWEEEEEN
----RAAAAAA
!!!!
FLY, MONSTER
!!!!!
CAPSULE
9
NO!! DON'T FALL NOW!!
BOUNG

HUH ?!
GUESS I GOTTA DO IT MYSELF!!
HWAA
OKAY, STAFF--
DO YOUR STUFF!
fwungg
HAVE A LITTLE NYOIBŌ...
BWAK
HYAH-- !!!!

SEE? ALL'S SWELL THAT ENDS SWELL!

WHAT'S SO ***SWELL*** ABOUT PEEING MY ***PANTS*** ??!!

REMEMBER YOUR CHINESE FAIRY TALES? YOU DON'T? NOT EVEN THE IMPISH ***MONKEY KING*** *AND HIS MAGIC STAFF, THE* ***NYOIBŌ****? OH, WELL... DROP IN NEXT TIME AND YOU'LL LEARN...*

NEXT: MY BALLS ARE MISSING!

Tale 2 • No Balls!

IN HER QUEST FOR THE SEVEN DRAGON BALLS THAT WILL GRANT HER FONDEST WISH, BULMA HAS ENLISTED THE HELP OF THE STRANGE CREATURE NAMED SON GOKU...

I GET THE SOFT LEAVES FOR MY BED!
...AS IF.
DO YOU REALLY THINK I AM GOING TO SLEEP OUTSIDE ?!
bmp

WHAT ELSE? I DON'T SEE NO HOUSES AROUND HERE...
CAPSULE TIME!

NO WAY! YOU'RE NOT GONNA POP A HOUSE OUTTA THOSE WHATCH-AMA-CALLITS!
PLEASE... THEY'RE "HOIPOI CAPSULES."

THAT LOOKS LIKE A NICE, LEVEL SPOT...
BETTER CLEAR OUT, MONKEY-BOY!
SSHOOOM

HOI!
POI!
BOMB!!

Ta-DAAAAA
AH! HOW LOVELY!
1
HOIPOI CAPSULE

COLD ENOUGH TO COME IN YET!?
A-ARE YOU *S-S-SURE* YOU'RE NOT A WITCH?!

WELL? STILL LUSTING AFTER THOSE *LEAVES*?
......

SPOP!
CLAP ON!
SPOP!

WAK!! YOU ARE A WITCH! YOU TURNED NIGHT INTO DAY!
YOU DON'T EVEN KNOW ABOUT LIGHTS? YOU HAVE A LONG WAY TO GO, TARZAN...

WATCH THIS!
FLIK

TWONGA TWONGA
BOOM BOOM
!?
HEH HEH HEH HEH HEH HEH...
!?
!?

HEY, GET OUTTA THAT BOX, YOU MIDGET!
YURRGH... YOU'RE STINKING UP THE JOINT...
YOU'RE TAKING A BATH BEFORE WE EAT!
TOK TOK

"BATH"? WHAT'S A "BATH"?
EEEW, YOU'RE KIDDING!!!

?
WILL YOU AT LEAST COVER UP?!!

GUESS I GOTTA HELP YOU. C'MERE!!

...OKAY, OTHER SIDE.
HUH ?

WH-WHAT'S THAT? IT FEELS WEIRD!
OH, SHUT UP!! DO YOU KNOW HOW MANY GUYS DREAM OF ME GIVING THEM A BATH?!
WHAT A WASTE OF MY BABE-ITUDE...

TAKE IT OFF! IT'S IN THE WAY!
OWW! DON'T PULL!

I CAN WASH MY OWN BUTT!
FWIP
.....

WHAT AN IDIOT! YOU ACTUALLY ATTACHED THIS STUPID, PHONY TAIL TO YOUR BUTT?!
WHAT PHONY TAIL?

EEEE-
YAAA!!!
eep!

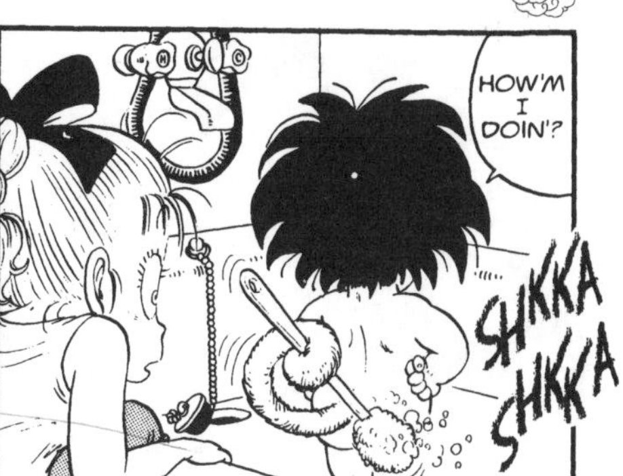
HOW'M I DOIN'?
SHKKA SHKKA

Y-Y-YOU R-R-REALLY H-H-HAVE A T-T-TAIL...!!!
I DIN' THINK YOU'D BE SURPRISED...
--OH, RIGHT! YOU DON'T HAVE ONE, HUH?
GUESS IT'S JUST GUYS.

BUT WAIT A MINUTE... MY DEAD GRAMPA WAS A GUY... BUT HE DIDN'T...
YOU SEE?! YOU SEE?! NORMAL GUYS DON'T HAVE TAILS!

GUYS HAVE...? NO, NO, THEY CAN'T...! BUT... IT'S NOT LIKE I'VE REALLY SEEN A GUY'S NAKED BUTT BEFORE...
I KNEW THEY HAD SOME-THING IN FRONT, BUT...

O'COURSE, GRAMPA WAS KINDA WEIRD...
--YOU'RE THE ONE WHO'S WEIRD !!!

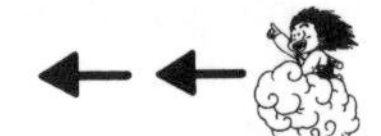

OH, WELL! WHO CARES?
......
I TAKE IT BACK... "WEIRD" DOESN'T EVEN COME *CLOSE*...

IS HE FOR *REAL*? HE ACTS LIKE *I'M* A WITCH OR SOME-THING...
...WHEN HE'S TOTALLY LIKE SOMETHING THAT JUMPED OUT OF A HORROR M...

B-LOOSH!

WHADDA YOU THINK YOU'RE *LOOKIN'* AT?!!!

...SO INSTEAD OF A TAIL, YOU'VE GOT AN EXTRA *BUTT*?
IT'S NOT A *BUTT*, YOU IDIOT!! THEY'RE *BOOBS*!! AN' WHEN YOU'RE A LITTLE OLDER YOU'RE GONNA THINK MINE ARE *INCREDIBLE*!!

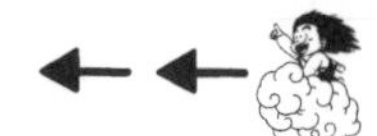

YEESH...!
HOW OLD ARE YOU ANYWAY, KID?

HOW OLD AM I?
14.

EEE-YAA!!
EEE-YAAA!!
VOYEUR!!
PERV--!!
YOU'RE ONLY TWO YEARS YOUNGER THAN *ME*!!!
TONG
!?
!?

HWRRR
NEXT TIME YOU PULL THAT, I'M CALLIN' THE COPS!!
I'M STARVIN'.
GROWL..

?
THIS IS FOOD?

THIS "BREAD" STUFF IS ALL SOFT AND NASTY!
AND THE SOUP'S *BITTER*...
--IT'S *COFFEE*, MORON! MAYBE IF YOU'D EVER LEARNED HOW TO *EAT* YOU WOULDN'T BE SUCH A SHRIMP!

I'M GONNA GO GET YOU SOME *REAL* FOOD!
HUH? WHAT? YOU'RE GOIN' OUT?

I'LL BE RIGHT BACK!

AWOOOOOO...

I'M HO-O-O-O-OME!!
THAT WAS QUICK...

!!
I CAUGHT A WOLF!
AN' A CENTIPEDE FOR FLAVOR!

EEEE-YAAA-AAAA !!!!

WE'RE SLEEPIN' APART?

W'LL, DUH!

AN' IF YOU TRY ANY-THING, YOU'RE DEAD!

WHEE-HEEE! THIS "FUTON" THING IS GONNA BE *FUN*!

AND I HAVEN'T SLEPT WITH SOMEBODY F'R *WAY* TOO LONG!

"SLEPT... *WITH*"...? YOU HAVE *GOT* TO BE JOKING! HERE'S YOUR BLANKET...AND HERE'S THE *FLOOR*.

boing boing

BUT I ALWAYS USED GRAMPA AS A PILLOW... IT WAS SO SOFT AND COMFY...

YOU AREN'T USING *ME* FOR A PILLOW, FREAK!!

SO IT WAS JUST YOU AND YOUR GRAND-FATHER, RIGHT?
WHAT HAPPENED TO YOUR PARENTS ?
I DUNNO.

I GUESS THEY ABANDONED ME IN THE MOUNTAINS WHEN I WAS A BABY.
THEN GRAMPA FOUND ME AND DECIDED TO KEEP ME!
HEH HEH HEH HEH...

HOW CAN YOU LAUGH ABOUT THAT...?
THEY PROB'LY ABAN-DONED YOU 'CAUSE YOU HAD A TAIL...

WERE YOU ABANDONED 'CAUSE YOU HAVE A BUTT ON YOUR CHEST?
I TOLD YOU, IT'S NOT A BUTT!!!
AND WHO SAYS I WAS ABANDONED ?!!!

I JUST HAPPEN TO BE ON SUMMER VACATION FROM SCHOOL--AND I'M TAKING ADVANTAGE OF IT!
I'VE ONLY GOT ANOTHER 30 DAYS TO FIND THE REST OF THE DRAGON BALLS! I DON'T HAVE ALL YEAR LIKE YOU!

ZZNXX ZZNXX
.....
RRRG... IF YOU'RE GONNA ASK QUESTIONS, AT LEAST WAIT FOR THE ANSWERS... !

TWI
TWI
TWI!
CHIRRUP
CHIRRUP
?
SHLMP SHLMP
NNH... ? WHA... ?
NNN-YAAAW... !
HUH ?

BUT I CAN SURE GIVE IT A TRY!

WHOA !
WELL, HER PILLOW'S NOT AS **BIG** AS GRAMPA...

...?
PAT PAT

?

KNK

!!

ZRRRR

EEEEYAAAA!

--GEEZ, YOU FREAKED ME OUT! STOP HAVING NIGHTMARES, WILL YOU?!!

SHLMP

!?

...AND SO BULMA SIGHS IN RELIEF, HER GREATEST FEAR AVERTED...BUT PERHAPS SHE SHOULDN'T RELAX QUITE ***YET***...

NEXT: SEA MONKEYS!

Tale 3 • Sea Monkeys

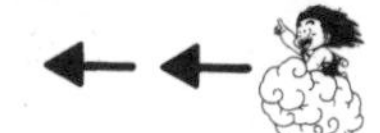

plip plip
BUT WHAT DID YOU "MISS"?
--NOTHING, STUPID!!

...OH, FORGET IT. WANT SOME?
THAT BITTER SOUP?! UGH, NO THANKS !!

WHAT I NEED IS EXERCISE !

HAIIII-YAAAA !!!
DM DM DM

HO !!

YA !!!
KRIIII

GLUMP

WHAT?

WHAT?

HUH ?!

Y-Y-YOU REALLY *DID* TURN INTO A TURTLE... !!
DEAR ME...WHAT A FRIGHT...
HUFF HUFF

WHAT ARE YOU BABBLING ABOUT ?
NOW WHAT ?

IT'S ALL BECAUSE YOU WERE SO ***SLOW***!!
?

IT'S NOT YOU?
AS *IF* !!

HUH ?
HUH ?
WHAT'S WITH THE TURTLE?!

IT LOOKS LIKE A SEA TURTLE...
...BUT WHAT'S IT DOING SO FAR INLAND... ?

PARDON ME, BUT IF I MIGHT TROUBLE YOU FOR A BUCKET OF SALT WATER... AND A SPOT OF SEAWEED, BESIDES...
NOT EXACTLY SHY, ARE YOU...?

GLMP GLMP

AHH...THANK YOU...THANK YOU SO MUCH!

I SHOULD EXPLAIN... YOU SEE...

...I'M A TURTLE.
AND WHAT AM I... *BLIND*?!!

I'M A SEA TURTLE, TO BE PRECISE... BUT I WENT GATHERING MUSH-ROOMS, DON'T YOU KNOW, AND... WELL, DASH IT ALL! I TOOK A WRONG TURN!
I'VE BEEN WANDERING ABOUT FOR THE PAST YEAR, HOPING TO FIND MY WAY BACK TO THE SEA...

WOW!
BUT YOU'RE GOING IN EXACTLY THE WRONG DIRECTION!
AND YOU'VE GONE A LONG, *LONG* WAY!

THE SEA'S TO THE SOUTH... ABOUT 120 KILOMETERS!
120...?! OH DEAR, OH DEAR...
MAP

HEY, YOU WANT US TO TAKE YOU TO THAT "SEA" THING?!
WOULD YOU REALLY?! OH, JOLLY!!

WHAT ARE YOU, NUTS?!!
WE'VE GOT 30 DAYS LEFT!! WE CAN'T BE WASTING TIME ON TURTLES!!
YOU'D RATHER WASTE IT BRUSHIN' Y'R HAIR?

LOOK, IT'S NOT OUR RESPONS-IBILITY!!
WE'VE GOT OUR OWN QUEST!!
THEN I'LL GO WITH-OUCHA.

FINE, DO WHATEVER YOU WANT!!! BUT DON'T EVER DARKEN MY HOI-POI DOOR AGAIN!!!

OOMPH!
I AM SORRY, OLD BOY...
NYAAHH!!

I MEAN IT! NEVER SHOW YOUR FACE AGAIN!
DM DM DM

WHO NEEDS YOU?!!

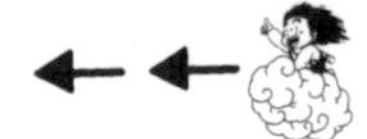

--HEY, WAIT *UP*, YOU GUYS!!!

YOU CAN'T DO IT *WITH-OUT* ME!!!

BIIIIOOOM

HUH...? WHAT ABOUT NEVER SHOWING MY FACE...?

I'M JUST TOO NOBLE FOR MY OWN GOOD, OKAY?

OH-HO, YOU GOT SCARED ALL ALONE, HUH?

SHOWS WHAT YOU KNOW...ALL YOU ARE TO ME IS A DRAGON BALL, DOOFUS!

HUP TWO THREE FOUR...
BIIIIIN...
HEH HEH HEH... WAITERS ON WHEELS, EH...?

hYa
HALT!!
HUH?

AND HOW DID YOU KNOW THAT SEA TURTLE...
...IS MY FAVORITE DISH! WA HA HA!

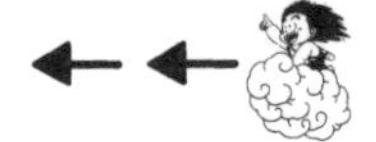

AKK! GIVE IT TO 'IM, PEE-WEE!
GIVE 'IM THE TURTLE, GIVE 'IM THE TURTLE!!!
BLEH!

OH-HO!
A WISE GUY, EH? JUST GIVE ME THE REPTILE, SONNY...
...AND I MIGHT LET YOU LIVE!

WHAT'S WRONG WITH YOU?!! GIVE 'IM THE STUPID TURTLE!!!
THE WORLD'S FULL O' TURTLES!!!
NYAH, NYAH! FOOEY ON YOUEY!
SO...YOU WANNA BE MY APPETIZER, EH...?

WELL, I DO AIM TO PLEASE...
FWOMMP
YOU BETTER GET OFF...

HYAH!!!!
VSSSHHHHH
GONG

YOU'RE A QUICK LITTLE MONKEY, I'LL GIVE YOU THAT...
HEH HEH HEH HEH...

--BEHIND YOU !
TOP

HEH HEH HEH...
HOP ON!! LET'S GO!!!
NOW'S OUR CHANCE !!!

YOO HOO !
ARH!!!

HYOH!!!
FWAH

ROCK...
SCISSORS...
TMP
...PAPER!!!!
BWEK
LATER!
NN... GAAH...

*AN IN-JOKE REFERENCE TO THE SETTING OF *DR. SLUMP*, TORIYAMA'S *SECOND* MOST FAMOUS SERIES.--ED.*

MUST BE PRETTY ROOMY, HUH?
HOW CAN I EVER THANK YOU?!
REALLY, I SAY, SUCH GENEROSITY MUST ***NOT*** GO UN-REWARDED!!

COULD YOU WAIT THERE FOR JUST A LITTLE BIT?
I'LL BRING YOU BACK A LOVELY REWARD, REALLY!
REWARD?
I CAN'T WAIT TO SEE A ***TURTLE'S*** IDEA OF A REWARD...

YEESH. IF I KNEW WE WERE COMIN' HERE, I'D A BROUGHT MY SWIMSUIT!
GLEHH!! WHO PUT ALL THE ***SALT*** IN THE WATER?!!

HEY... WHAT'S THAT...
HUH?

Aloha~!

SORRY TO KEEP YOU WAITING !!

NEXT: HEY! GOKU! GET OFFA MY CLOUD!

Tale 4
They Call Him…the Turtle Hermit!

...OKAY, SO SON GOKU HELPS A TURTLE. THE TURTLE WANTS TO GIVE HIM A REWARD. SWELL. EXCEPT THE "REWARD" IS--

COME TO ME... IMMORTAL PHOENIX !!

HHSSSHHHH...
...
WAS THAT "IMMORTAL"... OR "INVISIBLE" ?
?

I WAS GONNA ASK HIM TO GRANT YOU IMMORTALITY... BUT I GUESS WE BETTER SCRATCH THAT...
--I'VE GOT IT!
THIS IS EVEN BETTER !

SIR...IF YOU'LL RECALL THE UNPLEASANT-NESS WITH THE TAINTED BIRD SEED...
GAAA, THAT'S RIGHT!! WE LOST THE POOR FELLER...
THE "IMMORTAL PHOENIX"... DIED?

COME TO ME...
...KINTO'UN !!

I-I-IT'S A CLOUD !!
HYOOOOOOO...
--PHEW !
WAGGA !!

HOW DO YOU EAT IT?
YOU DON'T EAT A MAGICAL CLOUD !!

YOU RIDE IT, BOY.
IT'LL TAKE YOU WHEREVER YOU DESIRE !

SKREEECH!
THIS IS KINTO'UN...
...AND I GIVE IT TO YOU!

WOW, Y'MEAN IT'LL REALLY FLY ME?!
THAT'S THE TICKET, BOY!
BUT...UNLESS YOU'RE PURE OF HEART, IT'LL NEVER EVEN LET YOU ON! THIS CLOUD'S GOT STANDARDS!

HEY, WHY DOES A "TURTLE HERMIT" HAVE A MAGIC CLOUD? I MEAN, WHERE'S THE LOGIC?
DEAL WITH IT.

HERE...
--WATCH THIS !

EEE-YAAA! MY HIP!!
M-MASTER, HOW CAN THIS BE...?

SHHHPP
GRAK!

LET ME TRY !!
PYONG

BWA-HA-HA-HA-HA !!!
SURELY IT'S DEFECTIVE...
NEEDS A LITTLE MYSTICAL TUNE-UP, MEBBE...

I'M ON A CLOUD! I'M ON A CLOUD!
IT SEEMS... FIXED, SIR...
MAYBE JUST A POWER-SURGE...

GO, CLOUD !!

WHOO !!
TUP
HUH ?

WA-HOOO!!!
HYOOOONNNN...

HEY, OLD TIMER, HEY!!
EH?
GIMME ONE TOO!!
GIMME ONE TOO!!

Y'SAID THE GIRLIE DIDN'T HELP YOU?
NO SIR, I DARE SAY!
HEY! WHO GAVE YOU THE SALT WATER, HUH?!

WELL, I'VE ONLY GOT THE ONE MAGIC CLOUD... BUT...
I S'POSE THERE IS SOMETHIN' ELSE I COULD GIVE YOU, IF...

...IF YOU L-L-LET ME...
...P-P-PEEK AT YOUR P-P-PANTIES!!

"MY P-P-PANTIES"?!
NOD NOD

I SAY, SIR! REALLY, NOW! I MEAN, YOU KNOW, REALLY!
CUT ME SOME SLACK! IT'S HARD BEIN' THE TURTLE HERMIT! I DESERVE THE OCCASIONAL PANTY-PEEKIN'!

WELL, NOW WE KNOW WHY THE CLOUD...
OH, SHUT UP!!

WELLLL... I GUESS...
IF IT'S ONLY MY PANTIES...

FWIP

PUH PUH PUH PUH PUH PUH

LOOK FAST !!!

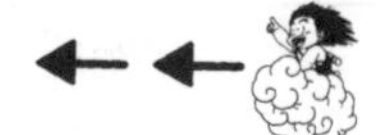

HEY!! HEY!!
LEMME SEE !!
WHAT? MY SHORTS ?!

OH, GET REAL!! THE THING HANGING FROM YOUR NECK!!
Y'MEAN THIS OLD THING...?

PURTY, AIN'T IT? SKIMMED IT OFF THE OCEAN FLOOR 'BOUT A HUNDRED YEARS BACK AND PUT IT IN A NECKLACE...
D- DON'T TELL ME... IT'S A...

--YO, GOKU !!!
GETCHER MONKEY-BUTT DOWN HERE! NOW!!
?

WHAT'S UP ?
LOOK AT THIS!! DO YOU SEE IT?!

A DRAGON BALL !!!
THEN I'M RIGHT, RIGHT?! RIGHT?!!
"DRAGON BALL" ?

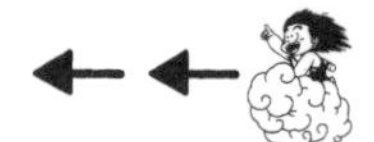

THERE'S THREE STARS IN IT! IT MUST BE THE "SANSHINKYŪ," HUH?
MY RADAR SHOWED ONE WAY TO THE SOUTH! THIS MUST BE IT!!
Y'MEAN THAT THING'S *VALUABLE*...?

NOW WE'VE GOT FOUR!!
WHAT *LUCK*!!! GETTING IT OUT OF THE OCEAN WOULD'VE BEEN SUCH A PAIN!
THANK YOU *SO* MUCH, OLD TIMER!

DID I SAY ANYTHING ABOUT GIVING IT TO YOU?
NOT IF I CAN MAKE SOME REAL *MONEY* ON IT...
OH, *DIDN'T* YOU?!
FWIP FWIP
PUH PUH PUH

OKAY, OKAY, OKAY...
sigh
WOO-HAAA!! WHOOPIE!!
I SHOULD'VE BROUGHT A CAMERA...
BYE-BYE!
WELL, *THAT* WAS WORTH IT, SURE 'NOUGH. SOME-TIMES...
...IT'S *GOOD* TO BE ALIVE.
...

SEE?!
NOW AREN'T YOU GLAD WE HELPED THAT TURTLE?!
IT WAS PURE, DUMB LUCK!

SOON AS I CHANGE CLOTHES AND CAPSULIZE THE HOUSE, WE'RE OFF!
ONLY THREE BALLS TO GO, RIGHT?
CAPSULE
AA1846

HEH, HEH.
WHAT AN AWESOME REWARD!

YAA-AAA-AAA!!!
MY PANTIES!!!!

HUH?! WHA HOPPEN?! WHA--?!
H-H-H-HOW CAN THEY BE *HERE* IF...

NO... DON'T TELL ME...
...

GNYAAH !!!!!

NAKED
NAKED
NAKED
NAKED
NAKED
NAKED
NAKED
NAKED
NAKED
NAKED
NAKED
I...I DIDN'T HAVE... *ANY-THING*...

AH, DON'T WORRY ABOUT IT!
YOU DON'T NEED THOSE PARTS TO SURVIVE!

!?
"THOSE..."?! WHAT... ARE YOU TALKING ABOUT...?
I SAW YOU DIDN'T HAVE 'EM. WHEN YOU WERE SLEEPIN'.

Y-YOU MEAN TO TELL ME... *Y-YOU* TOOK OFF MY PANTIES...?!
WHAT'S A "PANTIES"?

THESE !!!!
OH YEAH. I TOOK 'EM OFF YOU.

RAT-A-TAT-TAT-TAT-TAT...
OWW!!! OWOOO!!!
IF YOU *EVER* DO THAT AGAIN... I'M SHOOTING TO *KILL*!!
HEY, THAT *HURT*!
WHAT WAS THAT FOR?!
CAPSULE NO.1
BIII

HURRY, WILL YOU?

YOU'RE GOING OVER THE SPEED LIMIT!!!

OH, SHUT UP !!!

WHERE IS EVERYBODY...? IT'S LIKE A GHOST TOWN...

NO... I CAN *SENSE* SOMEBODY...

*A VILLAGE SEEMINGLY DESERTED IN THE MIDDLE OF THE DAY...PRESENCES "SENSED" BUT UNSEEN...WHAT THE HECK'S GOING **ON** HERE?!*

NEXT: OOLONG FOR TWO!

Tale 5 • Oo! Oo! Oolong!

CAN THIS EERILY SILENT VILLAGE BE THE RESTING PLACE OF THE FIFTH DRAGON BALL...?

NO, NO... I CAN *FEEL* 'EM...

YOU'RE NUTS...THERE CAN'T BE ANYBODY IN THIS PLACE!

BUT I'M SENSING ALL KINDSA PEOPLE!
I'M GONNA GO CHECK THIS OUT!
TMP TMP

DOOM DOOM
HEY!! I KNOW YOU'RE IN THERE !!
SHERMAN THE SHAMAN
WHY DON'T YOU ANSWER ?!

DOOR MUST BE LOCKED.
BULMA
OH, YEAH ?

BWAK

NOW IT'S OPEN !
KRII!..
NOT AFRAID OF MUCH, ARE YOU?
BULMA

HAI-YAA !!!
WHA-- ?!

CRAKK

OW... OW... OW... OW... OW... !!
GUH... GUH... GUH...

NO...
IT DIDN'T WORK... !
GTUNK

WHAT WAS *THAT* ABOUT ?!!

F-F-FORGIVE ME, LORD OOLONG !!!
I'LL GIVE YOU ANYTHING!! FOOD!! MONEY!! ONLY PLEASE SPARE MY DAUGHTER !!

HUH ?
OO... LONG... ?

YADDA YADDA
YADDA YADDA
I THOUGHT IT WAS WEIRD FOR HIM TO BE SHOWIN' UP THIS EARLY...
Y'MEAN IT WASN'T OOLONG? THANK GOODNESS...

S-SORRY ABOUT THAT, YOUNG FELLA!! I JUST FIGURED OOLONG WAS TAKING A BOY'S FORM... HEH HEH...
ARE YOU ALL RIGHT?
BULMA

SQUIP...

Pat Pat
EEEK!!

HMMM
?

L-LUCKY IT WASN'T, EH? HEH HEH.
IF THAT HAD BEEN ME, I'D BE DEAD RIGHT NOW!!
BULMA

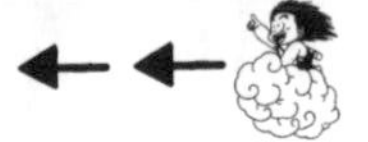

I GET IT... YOU'RE A GIRL!!

SSHHM
BULMA
PWAK

WHAT NOW ?!
NO "PAT-PAT" !!!
BULMA

? ?
ANYWAY... WHO'S THIS OOLONG YOU'RE SO FREAKED OUT ABOUT?
OOLONG... ! BRRR!

HE IS A HORRIBLE DEMON WHO HAUNTS OUR LAND...A VILE SHAPE-SHIFTER WHOSE TRUE FORM NO ONE HAS EVER SEEN! YESTERDAY HE CAME TO OUR VILLAGE...

...AND HIS EYES FELL ON MY DAUGHTER...
WOO-HAH!! SHE'S A KEW-TEE!! I'M GONNA MARRY HER!!
I'LL BE BACK TOMORROW AT NOON TO PICK HER UP, SO HAVE HER READY!!

HE'S A FIEND, WHO'S ALREADY KIDNAPPED OTHER VILLAGE GIRLS... TO DO WITH THEM WHO-KNOWS-WHAT...
...AND HE'S THREATENED TO KILL AND *EAT* EVERY VILLAGER... IF *ANY* OF US TRY TO FLEE OR RESIST HIM...

WHY DON'T YOU JUST BEAT HIM UP?!
ARE YOU KIDDING?! HE'S *HUGE* !!

WAAAIT A MINUTE...
RIFFLE RIFFLE...

HEY, MISTER...
...YOU EVER SEEN ONE OF THESE?
BULMA
EH ?

...? HMM...
NOPE... NOPE... NEVER SAW ANYTHING LIKE IT...

--WAIT !!
I'VE GOT ONE JUST LIKE IT!!

B-I-N-G-O !!!
YOU DO... ?

A LONG TIME AGO, MY OLD GRANNY PICKED IT UP FROM SOMEWHERE...
IS THIS IT?
YUP, THAT'S IT!!
FOUR... FIVE...SIX! IT'S THE "LIUSHINKYŪ" !!!
...?

BULMA
MA'AM, IF YOU'LL GIVE ME THAT BALL...
...I'LL TAKE CARE OF THIS OOLONG FOR YOU!

WELL, IT'S A LOVELY OFFER, OF COURSE, BUT...
...BUT DO YOU THINK IT'S A JOB FOR A SCHOOL-GIRL ?

BULMA
OHHH, NO! *I'M* NOT THE ONE WHO'S GONNA FIGHT HIM!!
HE'S THE...

PAT PAT

HEY! YOU'RE A GIRL TOO!!
OHHH, SONNY !!
...I *SAID*, NO "PAT-PAT"!!!!

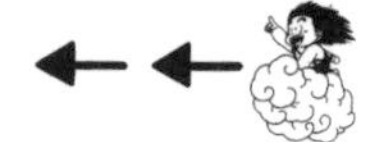

BUT...BUT EVEN IF YOU DEFEAT OOLONG... (FAT CHANCE)...
...WE DON'T KNOW WHERE HIS LAIR IS ! HOW WILL WE FREE THE OTHER GIRLS?

I'VE GOT A BRILLIANT IDEA! CAN I BORROW YOUR CLOTHES FOR A LITTLE WHILE?
HUH? MY CLOTHES... ?

WHY DO I HAVE TO WEAR THIS FLAPPY THING?!
IT'S YOU! IT'S YOU!
NOW LISTEN...YOU'RE GOING TO PRETEND TO BE THAT GIRL AND LET OOLONG TAKE YOU TO HIS LAIR. OKAY? THEN YOU BEAT HIM UP AND RESCUE THE GIRLS HE'S CAPTURED!

SHOOOOM
SHOOOOM

HE'S HERE !!
IT'S OOLONG !!!

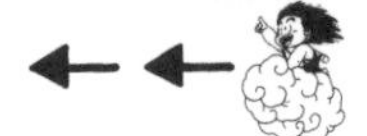

SHOOOOM
SHOOOOM
HEH HEH HEH! THERE'S MY CUTE LI'L BRIDE!! C'MERE, HONEY!!
SHERMAN THE SHAMAN

HUH? 'ZAT ALL YOU'RE BRINGIN' FOR YOUR NEW MARRIED LIFE? JUST A STICK?!
YEE-UP!!
NOW LET'S GET GOIN' TO YOUR LAIR!!

OH, *GREAT*, HE'S *ROLE-PLAYING*--!!
WHO'D EVER TAKE *HIM* FOR A TERRIFIED KIDNAP VICTIM...!?

C'MON, BABY, DON'T POUT!
I'M REALLY JUST A BIG SWEETHEART, Y'KNOW! *HEH HEH!*

SHIVERIN', HUH? YOU COLD?
BRRR!

NOT HARDLY...
...I'VE GOTTA *PEE!*

YOU'RE SCARED OF MY LOOKS, HUH?
--I KNOW!!

THEN HOW 'BOUT...
PRESTO!!!
BOMB!
...SOMETHING A LITTLE NICER?
OR DO YOU WANT A YOUNGER MAN?
WHOA...

HUH ?!

H-HEY THERE...
TEE-HEE!
MY NAME'S BULMA! AND I'M SWEET 16!

WHUH...
WH-WHAT'S YOUR BR-BRA SIZE...?
34-C !!!
poing!

34...C? WHOA...I COULD DO PUFF-PUFFS...!
PITIFUL, AIN'T IT?
B-BUT SHE'S 16...OLDER THAN ME...! 'COURSE, SHE DOESN'T HAVE TO KNOW...

WHAT A CHOICE! THE YOUNG 'N' INNOCENT 'N' NOT-SO-SCARY ONE...OR THE OLDER 'N' BIGGER ONE...!
MAYBE I SHOULD JUST TAKE BOTH! YEAH, THAT'S IT!
mumble mumble
HI-YEE!
OOOOO-LONG!

LOOKA MEEE!
LOOKA MEEEE!
HUH ?!
PSSS...
WHEW!

I CAN'T BELIEVE THIS! A YOUNG LADY LIKE HER...
HOW CAN SHE DO THAT IN PUBLIC?! COME TO THINK OF IT...
HOW CAN SHE DO IT AT ALL...?!

B-BUMP B-BUMP B-BUMP B-BUMP B-BUMP B-BUMP
PEEK !

GHEEE-YAAA !!!!
I SAW IT!!! I SAW IT!!!

YOU'RE NOT THE GIRL FROM YESTERDAY !!!!!
WOW !!
YOU FIGURED THAT OUT WITHOUT A PAT-PAT?! YOU'RE GOOD!!

YOU... YOU... YOU... !!
HOW DARE YOU TRY TO DECEIVE THE GREAT AND TERRIBLE OOLONG?!!'

PRESTO !!!!
BAKOOM!

NOW YOU SHALL SEE THE RAGE OF OOLONG!! THE RAGE-- AND THE ***POWER***!!!!

GLAK!

YOU TURNED INTO AN OX!

HEY, COOL!

stff stff

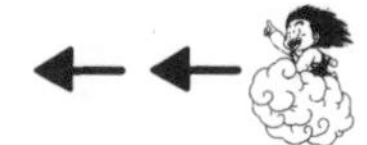

NEXT: SO LONG, OOLONG!

Tale 6
So Long, Oolong!

SUCH A DEAL! DEFEAT THE TERRIBLE DEMON **OOLONG** AND GET ONE FREE DRAGON BALL! SON GOKU CAN'T LOSE...CAN HE?!

NYEH HEH HEH HEH... LAST CHANCE TO APOLOGIZE, KID.

C'MON! YOU FIRST!

TIME OUT!!!
TIME OUT!!!
GALLUMP GALLUMP
HEY !

YAAA !!!
IT CAN'T BE!!

BOMB!

PWOOP...
AGE

GET BACK HERE !!
NO TIME OUTS !!

huff
huff
huff

AT LAST!! THE SECRET OF OOLONG!!

HE CAN CHANGE FORM AS QUICKLY AND AS OFTEN AS HE WANTS...BUT ONLY FOR FIVE-MINUTE PERIODS! AFTER FIVE MINUTES OF TRANSFORMATION, HIS MAGIC REQUIRES A FULL MINUTE TO RECHARGE!

WA-HA-HA-HA-HA-HA!!!

YOU DREAM THAT THE MIGHTY OOLONG WOULD *FLEE*?! I JUST TOOK A BREAK TO DESTROY *ANOTHER* VILLAGE, THAT'S ALL!!!

根 性

HUH?!

AH, NO SMART REMARKS THIS TIME, EH?!!
SURRENDER NOW, OR I'LL DUNK YOU IN THIS BOILING SOUP AND SLURP YOU UP LIKE A RAMEN NOODLE!!
YOU CHANGED AGAIN.
ARE YOU GONNA FIGHT, OR JUST PLAY DRESS-UP?

WHAT DID YOU--?!!
PLOOP

EEYOW!!!
MY THUMB!!! MY THUMB!!!!

YOU... YOU...YOU... YOU!!! YOU... YOU...YOU... YOU...!!
WHAT DID I DO?

ARE YOU SURE YOU WANT TO MAKE ME ANGRY?!
SNEAK SNEAK

GNNG...

PSHH
KONG

WAGGA
WAGGA
WAGGA!!!
GLEE-YAUGH!!!

WHAT ARE YOU DOING, CHILD?! RUN, RUN!!
EEP! OPP! NNNGH...! OOF! OOF!

WHAT'S *WRONG* WITH YOU?!!
CAN'T YOU CONTROL YOUR *KIDS* IN THIS TOWN?!!
...
FORGIVE ME!! FORGIVE ME!!
VSSH

HEH HEH HEH HEH...
THAT'LL TEACH *HER*...

HEY, TELL ME SOME-THIN'.
ARE YOU REALLY A PUNY WEAKLING?

WHAT?! N-N-NO!!!
I'M THE STRONGEST IN THE WORLD!! ASK ANY-BODY!!!
YOU DON'T SAY...

AND WHAT ABOUT YOU, HUH?! HUH?! HUH?!
HOW STRONG ARE YOU?!
WELL, MY GRAMPA TAUGHT ME KUNG FU.

K... KUNG FU...?
TH-THINK YOU'RE PR-PRETTY GOOD... EH...?

SO PROVE IT!
NNNNNKKHH...
SCRAPE...
CAN YOU BREAK THREE BRICKS WITH YOUR BARE HANDS?!
BRICKS?

I C'D DO IT...
...WITH ONE FINGER!

WATCH!
BRAKK

SEE?

...HEH...
HEH HEH HEH HEH...

PRESTO !!!
BTHOOM
WA-HA-HA-HA-HA-HA-HA-HA-HA!!!
ta-DAAA

FARE-WELL !!!
YOW !!
FWAP FWAP

...
WHAT TH'...?
WHAT IS HE...?
YIP

DON'T JUST STAND THERE!! GO CATCH HIM!!
IF WE DON'T FIND HIS LAIR, WE WON'T BE ABLE TO RESCUE THOSE KIDNAPPED GIRLS!!
OH! RIGHT !!

KINTO'UN !!!

BA-HOOOOOO
GO, CLOUD, GO!!
D'YA THINK HE'LL KETCH 'IM...?
NO SWEAT!
SOMEHOW... I THOUGHT OOLONG WOULD BE FIERCER...
WE WERE SO SCARED OF HIS LOOKS THAT WE NE'ER THOUGHT OF FIGHTIN' BACK...
AARGH!!
HOW EMBAR-RASSING CAN YOU GET?! I'LL NEVER BE ABLE TO TERRORIZE THAT VILLAGE AGAIN!!
SHHH
YOO-HOO!
THOUGHT YOU COULD GET AWAY, HUH?!
WAK!!!

BYUUUU

PR-PR-
PRESTO
!!!
BOM!

OH, NO !!
HYOOOOOOOO
I-I-IT'S ALMOST BEEN FIVE--
HSSSHHHHH

OOWAAAA

BOM!!
--MINUTES !!
HUH ?!!

SO... *YOU* WERE OOLONG ALL ALONG !!
...
B-B-BUT WHO...OR WHAT... ARE Y-Y-YOU... ?!

GMP

C'MON! *SAY* IT!
I'M... I'M... SORRY.
I CAN'T EVEN STAY MAD AT HIM...
THIS IS THE TERRIBLE OOLONG ?!

THEN TAKE US TO THEM! *NOW!!*
YOU SURE GOT TOUGH ALL OF A SUDDEN...

THOSE GIRLS'D BETTER BE ALIVE AND WELL!!
OH, *VERY* WELL...
"VERY"... ?

LLAGE
BULMA
HEY, THANKS !!
HERE'S THE BALL, AS PROMISED !!
MY, MY! WHAT A LAD!
AN' IF YOU TURN INTO AN ANT AND TRY TO ESCAPE, I'M GONNA SQUISH YOU! GOT IT?!
HOW DID HE KNOW... ?

AND HERE I WAS EXPECTING A CAVE...
HEH HEH... WITH ALL THE MONEY I EXTORTED?
WATCH IT, PIG!
BULMA
OOLONG'S LAIR
烏龍
SLURRRP...
PRECIOUS!! IT'S ALL OVER, AT LAST!!
PRINCESS!! MOMMY'S HERE!!
KITTEN!! DADDY'S COME TO RESCUE YOU!!
WHY DO YOU THINK I WANTED A NICE, SHY GIRL?
THESE CHICKS'RE WEARIN' ME OUT.
TAKE 'EM HOME WITH YOU... PLEASE!
...HUH?...
THIS SURE BEATS FARMING!
IF YOU'RE WORRIED ABOUT US, FORGET IT.

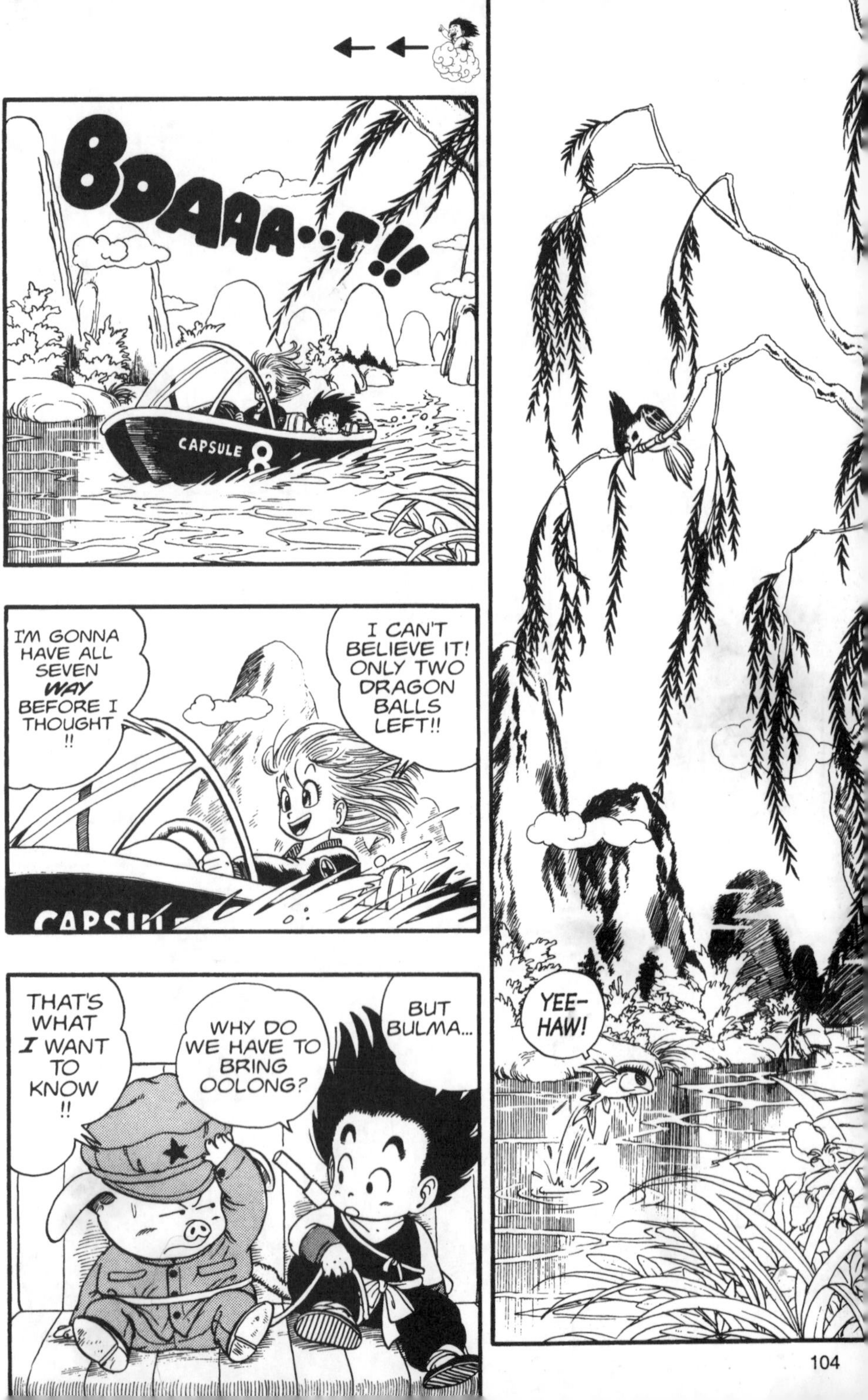

YEE-HAW!

BOAAA-T!!
CAPSULE 8

I CAN'T BELIEVE IT! ONLY TWO DRAGON BALLS LEFT!!
I'M GONNA HAVE ALL SEVEN *WAY* BEFORE I THOUGHT!!

BUT BULMA...
WHY DO WE HAVE TO BRING OOLONG?
THAT'S WHAT *I* WANT TO KNOW!!

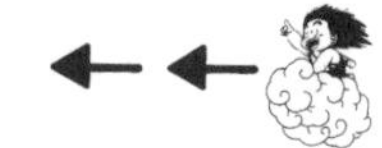

NEXT: DIM SUM AND SOOCHONG

Tale 7 • Yamcha and Pu'ar

EAGERLY TO THE SOUTH-WEST JOURNEYS OUR INDEFATIGABLE THREESOME... THEN, A LITTLE LESS EAGERLY...AND A LITTLE LESS EAGERLY...AND...

BOAAA...T

YOU'VE HEARD OF IT?
Y-Y-YOU DON'T *KNOW* ?!
TH-TH-THAT'S THE HOME OF THE TERRIBLE GYŪ-MAŌ, A.K.A. *THE OX KING!!!!*

HEY, NO PROB. GOKU'LL KICK HIS BUTT FOR US!
YOU DON'T KNOW THE *OX KING* !!
HE SOUNDS FUN!
CAPSULE

INCLUDE ME *OUT*!!!
BOM!
HEY !!

NYAH NYAH! BYE, SUCKERS !!
HE'S GETTIN' AWAY !!!

A FISH? WHAT A CHICKEN! NOW I'LL HAVE TO GO CATCH HIM!
WAIT, WAIT...

I HAVE A BETTER IDEA. NO NEED TO GET WET.
HUH ?
DON'T LOOK NOW...

?
?
?
K-PLOP
CAPSULE
8
8 CAPSULE

THIS'LL DO IT!
WHAT *IS* THAT?
FRESH PANTIES, THAT'S WHAT!!

FWAA
WHAT'D I *TELL* YA?!!

JERK !!

BOOAA··T!

PULL THAT FISH TRICK AGAIN, AN' WE KNOW WHAT'S FOR DINNER, GOT THAT?
OKAY, OKAY, I KNOW WHEN I'M BEAT.
BUT YOU COULD AT LEAST GIVE ME THE PANTIES...

I DON'T GET IT...
WAUGH !!

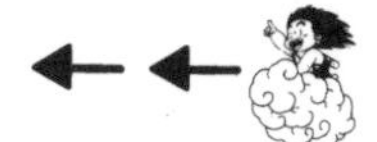

HERE.
TAKE THIS INSTEAD.
HUH ?

JUST A CRUMMY SWEETART?! WHAT A RIP-OFF!
MAKE YOURSELF USEFUL... AND YOU'LL GET THOSE PANTIES.

I WILL, HUH?
I'LL HOLD YOU TO THAT!
KORO KORO

HEY, I WANT SOME CANDY TOO!
UH-UH, NOT FOR YOU!
WAHAHA!! GIRLS ALWAYS LIKE ME BEST!

BBB BBB
WHA-- ?
PTTT!!
THE BOAT STOPPED TALKING!

AGH! WE'RE OUT OF GAS!

CAN'T YOU TURN INTO GAS, OR SOME-THING?
OH, YEAH, RIGHT.
MY FOOD TURNS INTO GAS...
8 CAPS

WE'VE GOT TO GET ASHORE SO I CAN TAKE OUT A GAS CAPSULE. SO TURN INTO AN OAR, OKAY?
AN OAR, EH...?
WHAT GOOD'S A BOAR?
8 CAPSULE

PRESTO !!!
BOM!!

ONE...
TWO...
BLASH BLASH
GLAA !!
GLUB !!
GENTLE, DUDE, GENTLE! I'M DELICATE!!
8 CAPSULE

ALL TIED UP!
GREAT.

OKAY, I MADE MYSELF USEFUL! NOW GIVE!
IF YOU THINK GETTING YOUR HEAD DUNKED IS WORTH A PAIR OF PANTIES, YOU ARE DE-RANGED!
JRBLE JRBLE
8 CAPSULE

IT'S... IT'S NOT HERE... ?
M-MY HOI-POI CAPSULE CASE...IS GONE!!

HEY, NO FAIR! YOU PROMISED! C'MON, JUST ONE PAIR!!
HUH ?!

A FISH!! GO GET IT!! PANTIES!! NOW!!!
DON'T BE RIDICULOUS. THE RIVER'S HUGE.

AAII-YAAA !!!!
I MUST'VE DROPPED IT IN THE RIVER!!!

WHAT'S WRONG WITH WALKING ?
EASY FOR YOU TO SAY, MR. FLYING CLOUD !!!
SNEAK SNEAK

HUH? WHAT'S GOIN' ON?
I LOST MY CAPSULES!!! THAT MEANS NO GAS...NO HOUSE...NO CAR...NOT EVEN A BIKE!!! I'M HELPLESS, HELPLESS, HELPLESS!!!

SO WHY DON'T YOU HAVE OOLONG TURN INTO A DYKE?
"BIKE"!! THAT'S *IT*!!!

OHHHH, OOOOO-LONG!!

GLAAA!!
HE'S *GONE*!!
I TOLD THAT JERK TO QUIT TRYIN' TO ESCAPE!!

hey Oolong, get back here!
ollie ollie oxen free!
HAH!! TRY TO TAKE *ME* TO FRY-PAN MOUNTAIN, WILL YA?!
NOT EVEN FOR *PANTIES*, BABE!

FOOEY! I THINK HE REALLY GOT AWAY!
HEH HEH HEH...
WELL, IF I REALLY *MUST*...

SWEEEEE! SWEEE-SWEE-SWEE...

*MANUFACTURER'S WARNING: SWEETROTS ARE ONLY FOR ONE MONTH PER DOSE.

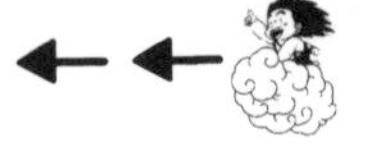

SWEEEE- SWEEE- SWEEE-
LEMME TRY.

NNNGH! I CAN'T BELIEVE I FELL FOR THAT! WHAT A DIRTY TRICK!
YOU SHOULD BE MORE LIKE ME!
I DIDN'T EAT ANY, DID I ?

OKAY, OOLONG.
YOU'RE TURNING INTO A MOTOR-BIKE!

GRGLE PFLSSHHHH
IT'S NOT FUNNY !!!

WELL... I GUESS IT'S BETTER THAN WALKING...

BULMA
MAYBE YOU THOUGHT I SAID "MOTOR-DORK"... ?
OH, SHUT UP...

GYAAUGH!!
KNSH

OH, GIVE ME A BREAK!!
I DON'T HAVE ANYTHING LEFT TO BREAK!! YOU'RE TOO HEAVY...AND NO MATTER WHAT SHAPE I CHANGE INTO, MY STRENGTH STAYS THE SAME!

I CAN ONLY STAY TRANSFORMED FOR FIVE MINUTES ANYWAY.
THEN I HAVE TO REST FOR A FULL MINUTE...
GUH.

BUT I'LL TELL YOU WHAT I'LL DO. WHEN I WAS A FISH, YOU GOT YOUR UNDIES ALL WET, DIDN'T YOU?
SO I'LL BET YOU'RE NOT WEARING ANY NOW. AM I RIGHT?
YOU DON'T WANT TO CATCH COLD, DO YOU?
C'MERE! TRY ME ON!!
BOM!!
YOU CALL THAT "USEFUL" !!!
PWAP
NNKH !!
I GUESS YOU'RE WALKING, AFTER ALL...

ZHEE
HUF
ZHEE
HUF
I'M... I'M GONNA DIE...!
WHAT'S TAKIN' YOU GUYS SO LONG?
IF I'M GONNA WALK, I WANNA DO IT FAST!

THERE'S... THERE'S NO WAY...AROUND IT...TO GET TO...FRY-PAN MOUNTAIN...
YEESH...I NEVER KNEW THERE WAS THIS MUCH DESERT...

I'M A CITY GIRL... REMEMBER...?!
I'M NOT SOME... FERAL BEAST-BOY...LIKE YOU... OKAY...?!
BULMA
WHEEZE
WHEEZE

ISN'T THERE... A HOTEL... OR AN INN... AROUND HERE SOMEWHERE...?
YEAH, SURE...THE "SHERATON WASTELAND."

CAN'T... TAKE IT ANY MORE...!
NOT ANOTHER STEP... TODAY...!
FUMP
HOW PATHETIC...

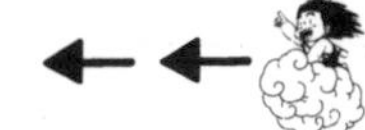

NOOOOO!! IT'S NOT FAIR!! IT'S NOT FAIR!!
I'M HUNGRY!! I NEED A BATH!! I CAN'T SLEEP WITHOUT A BEH-HEH-HED!!!
SPOILED ROTTEN, ISN'T SHE?
LOOK WHO'S TALKING

WHAT DID SHE SAY ABOUT A BED...?
...

I'M HUNGRY...
WE SHOULD REST, TOO.

HEH.

PYONG
KUNG PAO

LORD YAMCHA!! GAME! WE'VE GOT GAME!!
WHAT ?!

HOW NICE...
OUR FIRST CATCH IN A LONG WHILE...

A BOY AND A PIG, EH...?
THEY DON'T LOOK AS THOUGH THEY'D BE CARRYING MUCH CASH...
BUT THEY MIGHT HAVE SOME HOI-POI CAPSULES !

INDEED, PU'AR!! PREPARE THE JET SQUIR-REL!
YES, SIR !!

I'M STARVING TOO...
I'LL GO LOOK FOR SOME FOOD.

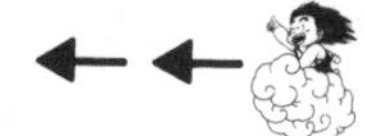

LET'S GIVE A WARM WELCOME TO THOSE BAD BOYS OF THE WILDERNESS, ***YAMCHA*** *AND* ***PU'AR***!! *AND HURRY--BEFORE THEY BASH IN OUR HEADS!!*

BASYUUU..!!

NEXT: ONE...TWO...YAM-CHA-CHA!!

Tale 8
One, Two, Yamcha-cha!

SMACK IN THE MIDDLE OF NOWHERE, SON GOKU, BULMA, AND OOLONG ARE SURPRISED BY A "WELCOMING COMMITTEE"-- YAMCHA AND PU'AR, THAT PLUNDERING, LOOTING DEADLY DUO OF THE DESERT!!!

WHAT... THE... ?

WHO ARE YOU?
I DON'T THINK I WANNA KNOW...

ME? I'M THE KING HYENA IN A LAND OF SCAVENGERS. THE NAME IS YAMCHA.
AND I'M PU'AR!

I DON'T USUALLY PREY ON BABIES...
...BUT IF YOU WANT TO LEAVE THIS DESERT ALIVE, GIVE ME ALL YOUR MONEY AND CAPSULES.

"PU'AR"...?
YOU DON'T MEAN..."CRY-BABY PU'AR"!?

GAH!!
OOLONG?!

YOU KNOW HIM...?
S-SORTA...IN MY FIRST YEAR AT SHAPESHIFTER SCHOOL, HE USED TO PICK ON ME ALL THE TIME...

...UNTIL HE GOT KICKED OUT FOR STEALING THE FEMALE TEACHERS' PANTIES!

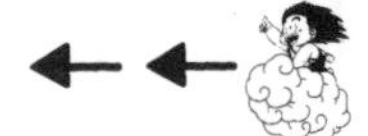

WEIRDO!! BULLY!! I HATE YOU!!
panties, eh?
IT WASN'T WHAT IT LOOKED LIKE!
YOU HAVEN'T CHANGED MUCH, HUH...?

WELL, IT'S NOT MY PLACE TO JUDGE OTHERS...
...ONLY TO STEAL ALL THEIR VALUABLES.

HEY! YOU'RE A TOUGH GUY, RIGHT?! REAL TOUGH?!
HUH? YEAH, I GUESS...

HAH!!
LISTEN, CHA-CHA, OR WHATEVER YOUR NAME IS! IF YOU THINK WE'RE GIVING ANYTHING TO YOU, YOU'RE DUMBER THAN YOU LOOK! NOW GET LOST BEFORE YOU GET HURT!

OH, REALLY? WELL, IF YOU'RE THAT EAGER TO SEE HEAVEN...
SHH...
YEAH!! KILL 'EM, LORD YAMCHA!!

VROOM
ALL RIGHT, GOKU!! HE'S ALL YOURS!!

HUH? WHY DO I WANNA FIGHT HIM?
WILL YOU PAY *ATTENTION*?!! HE'S GONNA *KILL* US!!!

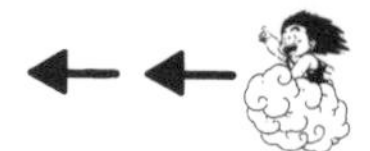

HEY!! WHY DO YOU WANNA KILL *US*?!
LET ME GUESS... YOU'RE THE SMART ONE.
COME ON, GOKU, *COME ON*--

I'M GLAD *SOMEBODY* HERE IS RELAXED...
SHNZZZ... GZAAXX...

HYAAAA!!!
WHOA !!

DYAAA!

PAH

HYOON

GROW,
STICK,
GROW
!!!

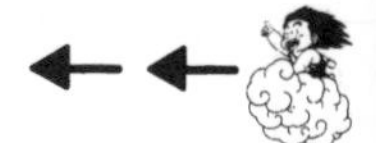

L-LORD YAMCHA... !!
WOO-HOO!! I *TOLDJA* YOU COULD DO IT!!

WHERE... DID YOU GET THAT STAFF... BOY...?
MY DEAD GRAMPA GAVE IT TO ME!!

I'VE HEARD OF ONLY ONE THAT LENGTHENS ON COMMAND... THE "NYOI-BŌ" OF LEGEND. TELL ME...
...WHAT WAS YOUR GRAND-FATHER'S NAME?!

MY GRAMPA'S NAME ?
HIS NAME WAS SON GOHAN !

AS I THOUGHT...
SON GOHAN WAS SAID TO BE UN-RIVALED IN A HOST OF MARTIAL ARTS DISCIPLINES...

EESH... EVEN *I'VE* HEARD OF HIM...!
AN' THAT'S REALLY *SAYIN'* SOMETHIN' !
THEN SON GOHAN HAD A GRAND-SON...
NOW I WILL REMEMBER... NOT TO LOWER MY GUARD...
I'M HUNGRY !

FIST OF THE WOLF FANG !!!
VSSH
HEH HEH...
IT'S BEEN TOO LONG SINCE I FACED REAL COMPE-TITION...
DOOM!!
HUH ?!

HYAA---!
BM
YAH!
YAH!
VSH
GM
VSH
BM
RRRRMMM...
RRRRRR...
BAKO-BAKOOM!!
YIPPEE, YIPPEE, YAMCHA!!!
OOOOH... I DON'T LIKE THE LOOKS O' THAT!!!

TH-TH-THAT WAS AMAZING, LORD YAMCHA!!
YOU'RE THE BEST IN THE WORLD!! I'M SURE GLAD I'M ON YOUR SIDE!

ffp

I'LL BE GOOD FOR YOU!! YOU'LL SEE!! I CAN TRANSFORM !!
KRAK KRAK

...YEAH!! THAT'S RIGHT!! I CAN TRANS-FORM!!

PRESTO !!
BOM!

BWAHAHAHAHA!!
BZZZZZZZZT

GET HIM, PU'AR!!
HE'S GOT !!

FLY SWATTER !!

SWAT
POM!
HELP ME !!!

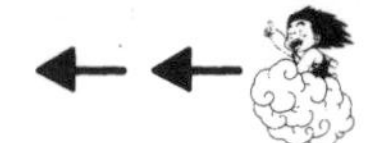

HEY, WE WENT TO SCHOOL TOGETHER !!!
OOO, THANKS FOR REMINDING ME!!

NOW.
IF YOU'VE HAD ENOUGH... GIVE ME YOUR MONEY AND CAPSULES.
M-MY THOUGHTS EXACTLY !!

RRGH... FOOEY...
MY EMERGENCY CAPSULE, YET...

HERE... SIR...
OH-HO! A "SIZE M" CAPSULE, EH?
NOT BAD... FOR A PUNK LIKE YOU. HEH... THIS SHOULD BRING US A NICE CHUNK OF CHANGE.

G-TONG
GONK...
I SAID... I'M HUNGRY !!

AND HITTIN' ME DIDN'T HELP!!
L-L-L-LORD YA-YA-YA-YA--
HUH! STILL ALIVE, IS HE...?

DO YOU WANT TO FEEL THE FIST OF THE WOLF AGAIN?

HYAAH!
VSSH
HOW 'BOUT MY FIST OF THE ROCK, SCISSORS 'N' PAPER?
!!
SCISSORS!
JAB
KRAK
ROCK!
FWAA
PAPER!!!

DONK
GOOOM

Y-
YOU...
LITTLE...
!!

I
GOTTA
STOP.
I'M TOO
HUNGRY
T'FIGHT
ANYMORE.
YOU
CAN'T
DO
THAT!!

RRRAAAAAR!!!

WAAH!!
YOU
MORON!!
YOU JUST
MADE
HIM
MAAAD!!
HEY...
WUZZIS...
?
RUB
RUB

BLUSH
TWITCH
TWITCH
TWITCH...

NEXT: ♪"SHIFTERS IN THE NIGHT..."♪

Tale 9
Dragon Balls in Danger!!

NIGHT FALLS...AND THE DEADLY DUO OF THE DESERT HAVE NOT YET VENTURED ANOTHER ASSAULT ON SON GOKU, OOLONG, OR BULMA, THE TERRIBLE ***GIRL***!! BUT IT IS AN UNEASY PEACE THAT SETTLES OVER OUR INTREPID TRIO...

OOLONG INC.
烏龍

IT'S SO TINY! IT DOESN'T EVEN HAVE A REAL BATHTUB!
OH, STUFF IT.

YOU BETTER NOT PEEK, PIGGIE!
HAH!

heh heh heh...AS IF A GUY LIKE **ME** NEEDS TO STOOP TO 'PEEKING'...

DO YOU HAVE ANY PJS?
HUH? OH. I'LL LEND YOU MINE.

YAMCHA'S LAIR
KUNG PA

THE SUN'S GONE DOWN...
IT'S TIME TO GET THAT CAPSULE.
B-BUT LORD YAMCHA...ISN'T THAT GIRL STILL WITH THEM?

HEH.
I HAVE A PLAN...

LISTEN CLOSELY, PU'AR. *YOU* TAKE THE SHAPE OF THE MONKEY-BOY, OR THE PIG...
....WHILE I GET MY HANDS ON THAT CAPSULE!
WHOA! BRILLIANT...

THEY COULD BE LURKING OUT THERE, Y'KNOW...
'SOKAY! I'M FULL NOW, SO I CAN'T LOSE!

SAY, WHAT ARE YOU TWO TRAVELING AROUND FOR, ANYWAY?
AND WHY DO YOU WANT TO GO TO... BRRR!... FRY-PAN MOUNTAIN!?
'CAUSE THERE'S A DRAGON BALL THERE.

A WHAT BALL ?!
I DIDN'T EVEN KNOW DRAGONS HAD--

...I GOT ONE HERE. I'LL SHOW YOU.

NEAT, HUH?

IT'S A HOUSE-WAGON.
SO THAT'S WHAT HIS "M" CAPSULE TURNS INTO, EH?
MAKES IT HARDER TO STEAL, DOESN'T IT...?

WE'LL JUST WAIT UNTIL THE GIRL'S ALONE... THEN YOU DRAW HER AWAY.

ALL RIGHT! SURVEILLANCE, FIRST!
SHOOOOM

LA LA LALA-LA-

I HEAR HER!
IF THE OTHER TWO ARE ASLEEP, IT'LL BE EASIER TO GET HER AWAY...

LET'S SEE...

!!

GUH-HUH... GUH-GEH... GUH-GUG-GUG-GUG... !!!
M-MY LORD!! WHAT IS IT?!

HUH...?
DID I JUST HEAR SOMETHING...?

A SIGHT, PU'AR...A SIGHT... BEYOND IMAGINING...!
HUH?

YOU'RE PULLIN' MY LEG!!

THE BRATS ARE AWAKE.
SOUNDS LIKE IT.

SO...IF YOU COLLECT ALL 7 OF THESE DRAGON BALLS...
...THE DRAGON WILL GRANT YOUR WISH?!
GREAT, HUH?

ANY WISH... AT ALL?
THAT'S WHAT SHE SAID.

AND HOW MANY OF THESE BALLS DO YOU HAVE NOW?
5! AND THE 6TH IS SUPPOSED TO BE AROUND THAT MOUNTAIN.

I'M STARTING TO GET IT NOW...AND THAT RADAR SHE WAS LOOKING AT IN THE BOAT...THAT TELLS YOU WHERE THE DRAGON BALLS ARE, IS THAT IT?
I GUESS SO.

PU'AR
!
POINT! POINT!
GOT IT!

VROOM

DID YOU *HEAR* THAT ?!!!
OH, YEAH !!

"ANY WISH WILL BE GRANTED..."
'SWHAT THEY SAID !!

WA-HA-HA !!
I WISH NEVER TO BE AFRAID OF *GIRLS AGAIN* !!!!

UM...NO DISRESPECT INTENDED, SIR...BUT SHOULDN'T YOU ASK TO RULE THE WORLD, OR FOR BOUNDLESS WEALTH OR...SOMETHING?

WHAT ARE YOU TALKING ABOUT? I CAN STEAL ALL THE MONEY I WANT...I'VE GOT NO USE FOR THE WORLD...
...BUT THIS BUSINESS OF GETTING ALL WEAK-KNEED AROUND GIRLS IS RIDICULOUS...

ESPECIALLY...

...SINCE I DREAM OF GETTING MARRIED !!

THOSE DRAGON BALLS... WILL BE OURS !!
YOU DREAM...OF GETTING MARRIED... ?

WELL, IT'S NOT THE KIND OF THING I CARE ABOUT...
HOW COME? WOULDN'T IT BE GREAT TO SEE A REAL DRAGON?

YOU MEAN... YOU'RE IN THIS JUST SO YOU CAN SEE THE *DRAGON*?!
UH-HUH!! AND I GET TO FIGHT, AND SEE DIFFERENT PLACES, AND...

YOU'RE SO WEIRD.
ALL I CARE ABOUT IS GIRLS.
THEN WHY DON'T YOU ASK THE DRAGON FOR A GIRL?

HEY! YOU'RE PRETTY SMART!
BUT WHY DO YOU LIKE *GIRLS*, ANYWAY?

YOU WOULDN'T UNDER-STAND.
BUT DON'T YOU KNOW? GIRLS HAVE *PIECES* MISSING! LIKE...

HUH?
DO YOU HAVE THE *SLIGHTEST* IDEA WHAT YOU'RE TALKING ABOUT?!

GONK

FINE! YOU'D BETTER HAVE MY CLOTHES CLEANED BY TOMORROW, THEN!

YES MA'AM!
WHY DO I LET THEM TREAT ME THIS WAY...?

--AND *YOU*! DO YOU CALL THESE PJS?! HOW AM I SUPPOSED TO FIT INTO THESE!
I TOLD YOU, THEY'RE *MINE*.
IT'S THOSE OR... NOTHING.
WAS IT S'POSED TO BE A SECRET...?

WHOA... SWEET!
COME ON, YOU TOO, DRINK UP.

GLP GLP...

WOULD YOU CARE FOR SOME JUICE TO COOL YOU DOWN AFTER YOUR SHOWER?
...WHAT'S "JUICE"?
HUH. I GUESS YOU'RE NOT ALL BAD...

DRINKING JUICE WILL MAKE YOU STRONGER!
REALLY?! THEN I'LL DRINK IT! AREN'T YOU HAVIN' ANY?

I DRANK MINE ALREADY.
OH, OK.
GLK GLK

ALL RIGHT... SO WHERE'S THE BED?
IT'S RIGHT UP THOSE STAIRS.
AM I STRONGER YET...?

AND YOU TWO SLEEP DOWN HERE--GOT IT?! IF YOU DO ANYTHING WEIRD WHILE I'M SLEEPING, OOLONG, I SWEAR, I'LL GIVE YOU SUCH A CASE OF THE--
--OKAY, *OKAY*!

TOO BAD HER PERSON-ALITY'S NOT AS GOOD AS HER BODY...

GNYAA GNYAA

NYEH HEH HEH HEH... IT SEEMS THAT THE SLEEPING POTION I PUT IN THE JUICE HAS TAKEN EFFECT...
NOW I CAN DO WHATEVER I WANT WITH THAT CHICK...I MIGHT EVEN... *HEE HEE*...FEEL HER UP...*HEH HEH HEH*...!

LOOKS LIKE THE GIRL IS UP AND THE GUYS ARE DOWN.
PERFECT! NOW... TRANSFORM INTO A KEY!

PRESTO !!
BOM!

HEE HEE HEE HEE...

KCHK

KRII...

VOOM

GZZZ GZZZ
EH ?!

THE COCKY FOOL...
BUT WHERE'S THE OTHER ONE...?

MAYBE HE WENT UPSTAIRS TOO.
ALL RIGHT, THEN. YOU TAKE *HIS* SHAPE--AND LURE *BOTH* THE OTHERS OUTSIDE!

PRESTO !!
BOM!

HOW THIS ?
PERFECT. JUST PERFECT.

HUH ?
I THOUGHT I HEARD SOME-THING...

THAT LITTLE IDIOT CAN'T ALREADY BE A--

WAAH !!

WHAT'S HE MADE OF?! THAT STUFF'S 'SPOSED TO LAST FOR HOURS!!

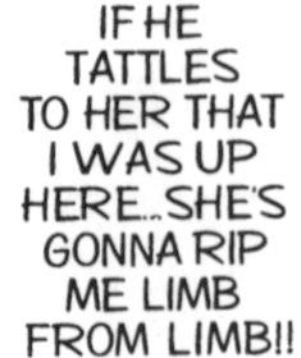
IF HE TATTLES TO HER THAT I WAS UP HERE...SHE'S GONNA RIP ME LIMB FROM LIMB!!

SHWAA
I-I'VE GOT IT!
I'LL COVER HER UP, AND--

PRESTO !!
BOMB!

OH... UM...
G-G-G-G-GOKU, HONEY...?
Y-Y-YOU'RE STILL UP...?

ERK
HUH? WH-WHERE'S OOLONG?

OO-OOLONG? H-HE'S NOT HERE! WENT FOR A WALK!! YEAH!!
OH! RIGHT!! RIGHT!!

UM...THERE'S SOMETHING I HAVE TO TELL YOU... S-S-SO CAN WE GO OUT-SIDE TOO...?
OH, SURE! NO PROBLEM! HAPPY TO!

ZZZ GZZ
SO... OOLONG WENT FOR A WALK, DID HE?
I'M RIGHT HERE... YOU DON'T HAVE TO YELL...

HMM... THAT'S STRANGE...
I'D HAVE SWORN THAT GIRL WAS THINNER...

--AH, WHO CARES? NOW'S MY CHANCE TO FIND THOSE DRAGON BALLS.
SHE PROBABLY KEPT THEM WITH HER... ON THE SECOND FLOOR...

HOW FAR DO WE HAVE TO GO JUST TO TALK?
MAYBE IF I CAN DITCH HIM...
J-JUST A LITTLE FARTHER, I PROMISE.

AHA!
THOSE MOUNDS ON THE BED...

HEH HEH HEH...IS THIS THEIR IDEA OF HIDING THEM?
THEIR TREASURES ARE MINE!!

FWA

WILL YOU JUST TALK ALREADY!! I'M BEAT!!
WELL, IF YOU INSIST...
SEE, THE THING IS...

BOM!!

NEXT: BULMA THE BUNNY!?

Tale 10
Onward to Fry-Pan...

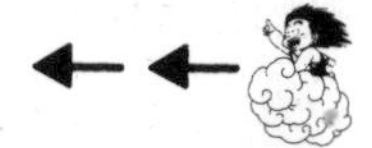

HE ATTACKED AGAIN LAST NIGHT?
NO! BUT HE SCARED ME SO MUCH I STAYED UP WATCHING ALL NIGHT!

OH... WONDER WHY I DIDN'T NOTICE...?
I NEVER SHOULDA SLIPPED HIM THAT MICKEY...
SHHH...

uggggh...
WHADDA HEADACHE...

HEY, OOLONG! DID YOU GET MY CLOTHES CLEANED?
AS IF I HAD NOTHING ELSE TO DO...

WHAT DO YOU MEAN, "NOTHING ELSE TO DO"?!
DO YOU THINK I'M GOING TO SPEND THE WHOLE DAY WEARING A SHEET?!

OOLONG WAS STANDING GUARD ALL NIGHT.
IN THIS PLACE THERE'S SOMETHING TO GUARD AGAINST?!

DON'T YOU REMEMBER?
THAT GUY FROM YESTERDAY!

OHHHHH... YOU MEAN THAT GUY!
WELL, IF YOU SEE HIM, SEND HIM RIGHT IN!

...
I GUESS IGNORANCE IS BLISS...

THERE IS ONE THING YOU COULD WEAR...IN THE CHEST ON THE SECOND FLOOR.
WHY DIDN'T YOU SAY SO ALREADY?!

DM DM DM...
I USED TO THINK I TOOK THE PRIZE FOR OBNOXIOUSNESS... BUT I BOW TO THE CHAMPION.

HEY, I'M HUNGRY!
I THINK WE CAN JUST ASSUME THAT.

GLMP GLMP
YOU'RE UP TO A MONTH'S RATIONS ALREADY!

OOOO-LONG!!!!
THIS BETTER BE A JOKE!!!!

FORGIVE ME IF I DON'T FEEL LIKE THE HEROINE OF A ***QUEST*** WHEN I'M DRESSED LIKE ***THIS***!!!
THAT DIDN'T SEEM TO STOP YOU FROM PUTTING IT ON...DID IT?

YEESH...
WHAT DOES A PARENT HAVE TO ***DO*** TO END UP WITH A KID LIKE YOU...?

WE GOTTA GET TO FRY-PAN MOUNTAIN! START DRIVING, OOLONG!
WHEW! MOMMA!
HUH? ME?!

WHO ELSE, IDIOT?!!
I HAVE TO SPEND MY MORNING WITH SKIN CARE AND COSMETICS!!
AND THE FACT THAT I HAVEN'T SLEPT...

...MEANS NOTHING...
CRUELTY TO PIGS, THAT'S WHAT IT IS...
BWOOM...

FEH!! THEY'VE STARTED MOVING...
WHAT SHALL WE DO...?

I *MUST* HAVE THOSE DRAGON BALLS...
...EVEN IF IT MEANS... WE HAVE TO USE FORCE!

PREPARE THE AUTOMATIC RIFLE-- THE PANZER FAUST-- AND THE "MIGHTY MOUSE"!!
YES SIR!!

BWOOM BBBBB...

DUM-DEE-DEE-DEEE-EEEE...
STUDLY BAD-GUY COME TO MEEEEEE...

"COME TO *ME*," SHE SAYS! NEVER MIND THAT IF HE DOES...
...WE'LL BE *PORK CHOPS*!
HEY, WHAT'S THAT?

WAAH!! IT'S HIM!! HE'S HERE!!

BURORO..!

烏龍

BFF

D-KOOOM

WAAAA !!!

WHERE?! WHERE?! WHERE IS HE?!

--NOW, PU'AR! STOP THE CAR!

ROGER!

KREE...

OO... OO... OO...
THAT... DUMMY !!

HEY !! WHADDYA THINK YOU'RE DOIN' ?!!

YOU'RE IN LUCK, LORD YAMCHA! IT SEEMS THE GIRL HAS FAINTED!
INDEED!

LISTEN UP, NOW...
HAND OVER THE DRAGON BALLS PEACEFULLY... AND YOU WON'T GET HURT AGAIN!

H-HEY! HOW DOES HE KNOW ABOUT THE DRAGON BALLS?!

I'M GIVIN' YOU...
...NOTHIN' !!

NO, YOU IDIOT!! THEY'RE NOT WORTH IT!! W-WE'RE GONNA BE KILLED!!
NYAAAA!

VMMM
NOOO !!

HEY! HE'S COMING TOWARDS US!
HEH HEH HEH... HOLD THIS AUTOMATIC RIFLE.
THIS LAD REALLY SEEMS TO WANT SOMEONE TO TEACH HIM A LESSON...

HA HA HA, SO YOU WANT TO TASTE MY "FIST OF THE WOLF FANG" AGAIN, EH?!! HA HA HA!!

YESTERDAY, I WAS HUNGRY !!
BUT RIGHT NOW... MY STOMACH'S FULL !!

BASH
!!
BISH
TAKE THIS !!
NO WAY !!
CHA
HO !!
FNNN
BWAAAA
HYAH !!
WAK

L-LORD YAMCHA!
Y-YOU... YOU...

DOMP!

AA!!

AIEE!! Y-Y-YOUR NOBLE TOOTH...!!
COME 'N' GET SOME MORE!
HUH ?!

J-J-JUST YOU WAIT...!!
YOU VILE... LITTLE...

NO NO NO NO!! NOT MY TOOTH!! NOT MY BEAUTIFUL FACE!!!
...?!

BRRROOO...
WHAT TH' HECK... ?
THAT WAS SO SHORT...

WHOA!! YOU ARE A-MAZING!! YOU ARE A STUD!!
I TAKE BACK EVERYTHING I SAID!!
HEH HEH HEH!

OF COURSE... IT WOULD BE BETTER IF OUR CAR WEREN'T WRECKED...
GUESS WE'LL JUST HAVE TO WALK...

C-CURSE HIM...
CURSE HIM FOR HIS POWER...!
A-ARE YOU ALL RIGHT, SIR...?
WE'LL HAVE TO REVISE OUR PLANS...
WHICH MEANS...?

WE SHOULD HAVE DONE IT THIS WAY FROM THE START... THEY WERE SAYING THAT ALL SEVEN OF THESE BALLS MUST BE TOGETHER, RIGHT?
THEN WE SHOULD STAY ON THEIR TAILS...AND STEAL THE BALLS AFTER THEY'VE GATHERED ALL SEVEN!! HA! I'M SO SMART!

GIRLS ARE SO LUCKY...
Y-YOU CAN LET ME CARRY HER... HEH HEH...

HUH ?!
BRRROOOO...
YOOOO-- HOOOO!!

GWAAGH !!
THEY'RE BACK AGAIN !!
HEY, GUYS!! HOPE THERE'S NO HARD FEELINGS!!

WE THOUGHT IT ALL OVER, AND Y'KNOW...
...THE WHOLE MESS REALLY WAS OUR FAULT !!
...HEH HEH HEH...

SO HERE... TAKE THIS CAPSULE AS AN APOLOGY !!
POOY
BOOM!

NEXT: THE HEAT IS ON!

Tale 11
...And into the Fire!

HAVING ESCAPED MORE-OR-LESS UNSCATHED FROM YAMCHA'S SECOND ATTACK, OUR HEROES PRESS ON IN SEARCH OF THE SIXTH DRAGON BALL. AND, TWO DAYS LATER...

ARE WE ***THERE*** YET?!

ALMOST, ALMOST, ALMOST...

YOW! NO WONDER IT'S SO HOT...!!
NO KIDDIN' !!
S-SO MAYBE WE D-DON'T HAVE TO GO, HUH? JUST LEAVE IT TO GYŪ-MAŌ!

"GYŪ-MA-WHAT"!? WHO THE HECK'S THAT!?
GYŪ-MAŌ THE OX KING, REMEMBER?! THE ONE THEY'VE NICKNAMED "THE EMPEROR OF DEMONS"...JUST BECAUSE HE'S SO NASTY!!

ALL WHO APPROACH HIS MOUNTAIN...
...COME TO HORRIBLE ENDS !!
KKK KKK

YOU MEAN YOU GET KILLED... ?
DUH

LOOK AT THE TOP OF THE MOUNTAIN. SEE THAT CASTLE IN THE FLAMES? THAT'S HIS!
IT OVERFLOWS WITH GOLD, SILVER, AND OTHER TREASURES THAT HE'S LOOTED FROM ALL OVER THE LAND! THOUSANDS HAVE TRIED TO STEAL IT, BUT HE KEEPS A CONSTANT VIGIL... AND NONE HAVE RETURNED ALIVE!

THAT BLAZE IS SO HUGE, EVEN AN OX FROM HECK LIKE HIM CAN'T GET THROUGH IT!

THEN THE SIXTH DRAGON BALL MUST BE IN THERE TOO...
IS THIS OX GUY THERE OR WHAT?
NO...HE GUARDS THE CASTLE FROM THE FOOT OF THE MOUNTAIN! IT'S ALL 'CAUSE THE MOUNTAIN FIRST CAUGHT FIRE WHILE HE WAS ON A PICNIC WITH HIS KID, SEE?

YOU SEEM TO KNOW A LOT ABOUT THIS.
WHAT, YOU MEAN THEY DIDN'T TEACH YOU ABOUT IT AT SCHOOL...?

ANYWAY, YOU GET THE POINT, RIGHT? LET'S GET!
BAM
AFTER COMING THIS FAR?! DON'T BE STUPID!

WHAT ARE YOU, ONE O' THOSE SUICIDAL TEENS I HEARD ABOUT?! I DON'T CARE HOW STRONG THIS GOKU JERK IS, THIS IS LIKE PITTING A...A MONKEY AGAINST AN OX!

THANKS BUT NO THANKS!!
UWIIIIN
HEY !!
HE'S RUNNING AWAY AGAIN !!

SWEEE-SWEE-SWEE...
SWEEE EEEE EEEEE...

YAAH!!
NOT NOW!!
NOT NOW!!
GURGLE GURGLE
VMM

OKAY!! OKAY!! I'LL DO ANYTHING!! JUST STOP IT!!
BLAAAAT
SHOOOM
PUT PUT PUT

AHA! THEY'RE MOVING AGAIN!
IT SEEMS THEY'RE DETERMINED TO GO TO FRY-PAN MOUNTAIN, NO MATTER WHAT...
RNN RNN RNN

HMMM.
THEN THE SIXTH DRAGON BALL MUST BE INSIDE THE DEMON'S CASTLE...

THE OX DEMON!? THEN THEY'RE NEVER GONNA GET IT!!
WHAT A BURDEN...

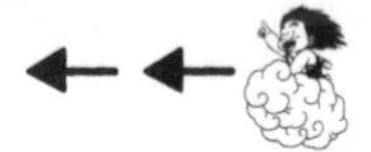

WITH THE FIRE *AND* THE SO-CALLED OX KING, THERE'S NO WAY, NO HOW.
I THINK WE BETTER JUST GO HOME AND...
WAIT... WAIT...
COULD IT BE THAT THAT MONKEY-BOY HAS AN "IN" WITH THE OLD BEAST...?
AFTER ALL, HE *IS* SON GOHAN'S GRANDSON...

AND I'VE HEARD THAT SON GOHAN AND GYŪ-MAŌ WERE ONCE BOTH DISCIPLES OF THE SAME INVINCIBLE OLD MASTER...
I THINK IT WOULD SERVE US WELL JUST TO SEE WHAT HAPPENS...

EEEEEE
WHA--?!

EEE-YOW !!!
DMMM DMMM

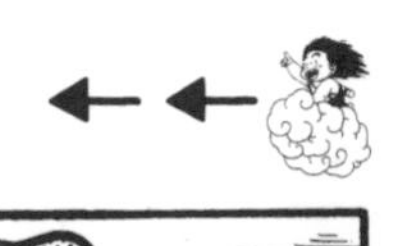

GIT, BOY!!

RRROAR

SHAA

...COME NO *CLOSER* !!

DONCHA *DARE*...

KACH
SHRRRRRRRRR
EEE-
YECCH
!!!
SPSHHH
DNG
AK
!!
BAKOOOOM!
BIIIIIIIIIII
GIT
OUTTA
HERE
!!!
OO, THIS
IS JES'
TOO DANG
FREAKY!!
SHKK

WAAAH!! THAT WAS SCAAARY !!
...
N-NOT EXACTLY THE PARALYZED-WITH-FEAR-TYPE, IS SHE...?
WH-WHO IN THE HECK...

WAK !!
UHH... H-H-HI...

YAAAA!! IT'S JES' ONE MENACE AFTER ANOTHER HERE !!
SHPP

HYAH !!
BIIIII
WAAH !!

YARH !!!

BONK

RGH!!

WHAT A STUPID DELAY...!

DMF...

PAP PAP

BUT WE HAVEN'T LOST YET! ON TO FRY-PAN MOUNTAIN!

B-BUT LORD YAMCHA...YOUR FEAR OF GIRLS... IT DIDN'T BOTHER YOU WHEN *SHE*--

...THAT *CHILD?!* DO YOU THINK I HAVE A *LOLITA* COMPLEX?

O-KAY, O-KAY...SO THAT'S THE CASTLE, HUH...?
B-BUMP B-BUMP B-BUMP

RADAR SAYS THE BALL'S THERE SOMEWHERE, ALL RIGHT...
IF I COULD FLY, IT'D BE NO PROBLEM...
Peep Peep

--YO! GOKU! THINK YOU CAN GO GET THE DRAGON BALL BY YOURSELF?!
HUH ?
I WON'T KNOW 'TIL I TRY, BUT...

KIN-TO'UN--!!!
WAAH!! I SA-A-ID, "DON'T SHOUT"!!
SHHHHH

LET'S GO, CLOUD!
YOU BETTER FIND IIIIT!!
AND DON'T TAKE TOO LONG!!

SO THAT'S IT...
THIS IS SO COOOL !!
WHOA!
GRRRR...
HOT HOT HOT !!
YEE-OWW !!
I MIGHT JUST BE ABLE TO...
SHHHH...
YARRGH!! HE'S SUCH A WUSS!!
SEE?! I TOLD YOU SO!! IT'S NO USE!! CAN WE GET OUTTA HERE NOW?!

BONG
EEP ?!
DOOOOOM
WAGGA WAGGA WAGGA !!!

WHAT'RE YEW DOIN'...
...HERE ON *MAH* LAND?
SWOPE
O-OH, J-J-J-JUST P-PASSIN' TH-TH-TH-TH...
W...WUH... W-WUH... ....
PSSSSS

NEXT: ***KAME***-ING ATTRACTIONS!

DRAGON

TITLE PAGE GALLERY

Here are the chapter title pages which were used when **Dragon Ball Vol. 1** was originally published in Japan in **Shônen Jump** magazine. Some were previously published in Viz's **Dragon Ball** monthly comic series; some have never before been seen in America!

Akira Toriyama
鳥山明 BIRD STUDIO

Tale 2 • No Balls!

The Monkey and the Princess…But They're Still Boy and Girl

ALOFT in the ULTRALIGHT of LOVE…Or ARE THEY?

Tale 3 • Sea Monkeys

Akira Toriyama
鳥山明 BIRD STUDIO

TOGETHER THESE TWO ARE UNSTOPPABLE!

ドラゴンボール
DRAGON BALL
Tale 4 •
They Call Him…
the Turtle Hermit!
ADVENTURE!
FA4
002116
79
BULMA
Akira Toriyama
鳥山明
BIRD STUDIO

DRAGON BALL
ドラゴンボール
Tale 5 • Oo! Oo! Oolong!
Akira Toriyama
鳥山明 BIRD STUDIO
BULMA
GIRLS CAN FLY HIGH, TOO!

Akira Toriyama
鳥山明
BIRD STUDIO

PUSUN PUSUN....

Tale 6 • So Long, Oolong!

DRAGON BALL
ドラゴンボール
Akira Toriyama
鳥山明
BIRD STUDIO
樂

ドラゴンボール
DRAGON BALL
Akira Toriyama
鳥山明
BIRD STUDIO
Come at me!
Whaddya got!?
You'll see...
an' you're not gotta like it!!
Don't mind me...
I'm along for the ride!
I gotta bad feelin' about this...
Hey, don't worry... I got it under control!

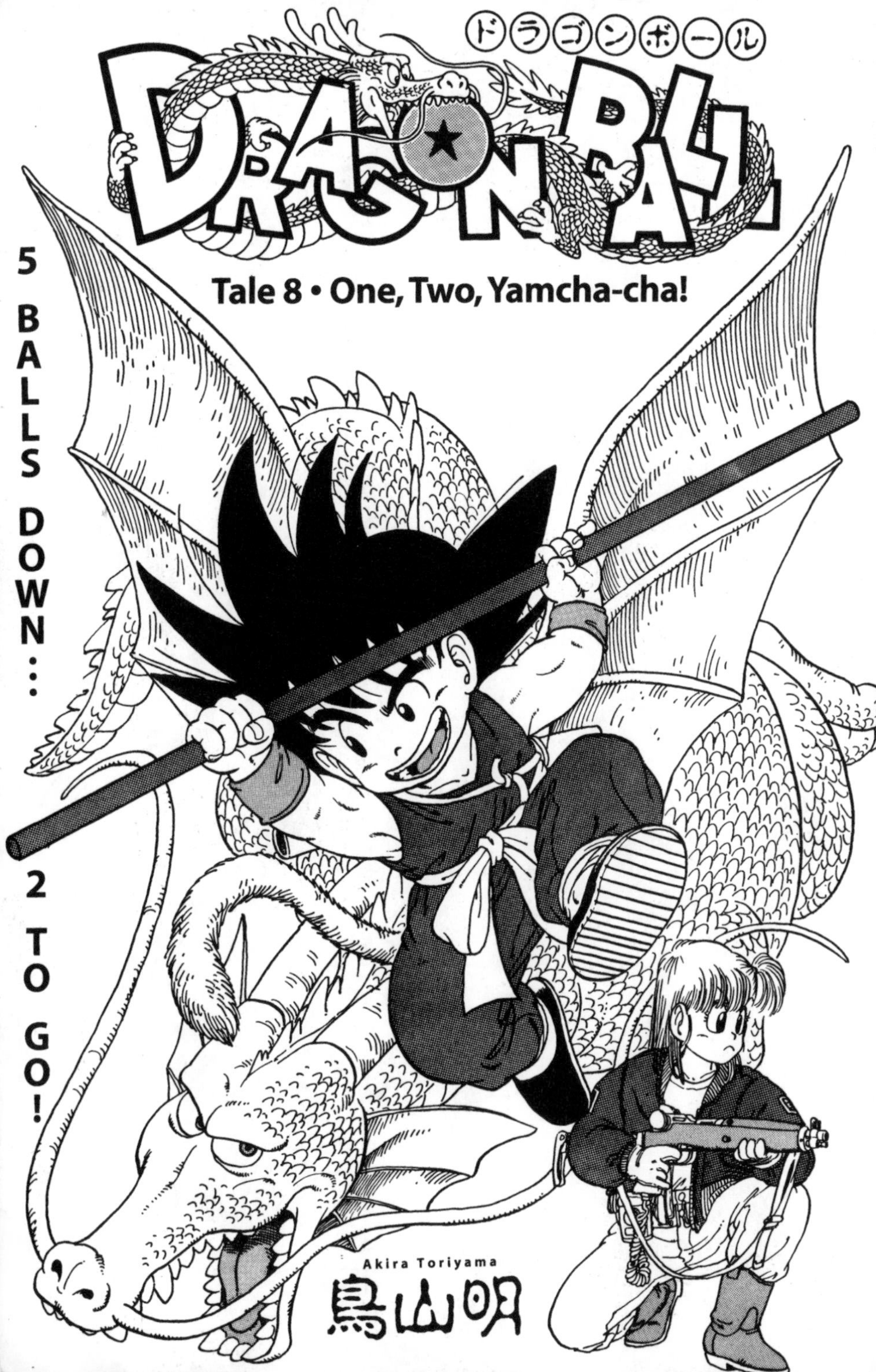
ドラゴンボール
DRAGON BALL
Tale 8 • One, Two, Yamcha-cha!
5 BALLS DOWN…2 TO GO!
Akira Toriyama
鳥山明

Akira Toriyama
—鳥山明—

ドラゴンボール
DRAGON BALL
Tale 10 • Onward to Fry-Pan…
Akira Toriyama
鳥山明
BIRD STUDIO
HERE COMES CHI•CHI!!!
This many down…
…this many to go!

The Most Active Book Around!

HAMTARO
little hamsters big adventures

PUNCH-OUT ACTIVITY BOOK

VIZ

PUNCH-OUT, BEND, & FOLD YOUR OWN HAM-HAM CLUBHOUSE!

STORY "BIJOU'S IN DANGER"

NO SCISSORS, TAPE, OR GLUE REQUIRED!

THUMP SEESAW SWAY SWING

COMPLETE SET OF HAM-HAM PUNCH-OUT FIGURES INCLUDED!

SLIDE WHOOSH WHIZ WHIZ WHEEL

Coming Soon!

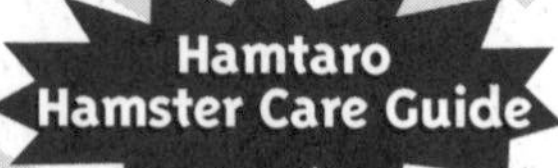

The Hamtaro Punch-Out Activity Book

Created by Ritsuko Kawai

Ticky-Tickying your way from